WITHDRAWN

THE CREDO SERIES

VOLUMES ALREADY PUBLISHED

THE CREDO SERIES

PLANNED AND EDITED BY
RUTH NANDA ANSHEN

Board of Editors

THE CHALLENGE OF THE PASSING YEARS

My Encounter with Time

BY

R. M. Mac IVER

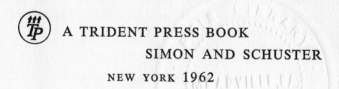

A TRIDENT PRESS BOOK

SIMON AND SCHUSTER

NEW YORK 1962

Prepared under the supervision of
POCKET BOOKS, INC.

CONTENTS

v

140599

THE CREDO SERIES

Its Meaning and Function

The Credo Series suggests that an epoch has come to an end, an epoch in which our best knowledge has been dimmed with boredom or darkened by destruction. We have felt for too long that this must be the very nature of life; this is the way life is, and to such a degree that life has consented to shrink from its own terrors, leading us to a deep apostasy of the heart and a crucifixion of our natural aspiration for experience and growth.

The absolute has surrendered to the relative. Our era of relativity, however, whether in science or in morals, does not allow us to assume that relativity implies an absence of ground to stand on, and therefore a relaxation of all effort toward foundations. "There is no firm ground," the dominant malaise of our time, this acceptance of non-finality, summons us to a heightened task. For the failure of formulated absolutes leaves the absolute requirement to evaluate again that uncaptured reality which contains and guides the total meaning of our existence.

The Credo Series hopes to unlock a consciousness that at first sight may seem to be remote but is proved on acquaintance to be surprisingly immediate since it shows the need to reconcile the life of action with the life of contemplation, practice with principle, thought with feeling, knowledge with being, and work, no longer a form of punishment as in the Judaeo-Christian tradition, but accepted as a way toward the growth and realization of the self in all its plenitude. For the whole meaning of self lies within the observer and its shadow is cast naturally on the object observed. The fragmentation of man from his work, the being of man into an eternal and temporal half, results in an estrangement of man from his creative source, from his fellows and from himself.

The symbol of *The Credo Series* is the Eye of Osiris. It is the inner Eye. Man sees in two ways: with his physical eyes, in an empirical sensing or *seeing* by direct observation, and also by an indirect envisaging. He possesses in addition to his two sensing eyes a single, image-making, spiritual and intellectual Eye. And it is the *in-sight* of this inner Eye that purifies and makes sacred our understanding of the nature of things; for that which was shut fast has been opened by the command of the inner Eye. And we become aware that to believe is to see.

Thus, it is suggested, there may be born a sharpened vision, which comes from seeing reality as the incarnation of associations and affinities with something beyond the visible self. For it is our hope to show the human relevance of ideas, the ways in which knowledge can help us to live in the immediate and real world by pointing to the confluence of man and his vocation, of subject and object, by reverencing the curious and mysterious metabolism between man and matter, the sacred nexus between the person and his work, and by asking whether the freedom now released through the creative energies of mankind will bring salvation or destruction, the answer to which will depend upon the aims we cherish.

The Credo Series submits that the universe itself is a vast entity where man will be lost if it does not converge in the person; for material forces or energies, or impersonal ideals, or scientifically objectified learning are meaningless without their relevance for human life and their power to disclose, even in the dark tendencies of man's nature, a law transcending man's arbitrariness.

For the personal is a far higher category than the abstract universal. Personality itself is an emotional, not an intellectual, experience, and the greatest achievement of knowledge is to combine the personal within a larger unity, just as in the higher stages of development the parts that make up the whole acquire greater and greater independence and individuality within the context of the whole. Reality itself is the harmony which gives to the component particulars of a thing the equilibrium of the whole. And while physical observations are ordered with direct reference to the experimental conditions, we have in sensate experience to do with separate observations whose correlation can only be indicated by their belonging to the wholeness of mind.

It is our endeavor to show that man has reached a turning point in consciousness, that his relationship with his creative self demands a clarification that can widen and deepen his understanding of the nature of reality. Work is made for man, not man for work. This Series hopes to demonstrate the sacramental character of work which is more easily achieved when the principal objects of our attention have taken on a symbolic form that is generally recognized and accepted: in other words, when there is an established iconography relating to the meaningful interpretation of man and his vocation. This suggests a "law" in the relationship of a person and his chosen discipline:

that it is valuable only when the spiritual, the creative, life is strong enough to insist on some expression through symbols. For no work can be based on material, technological or physical aspirations alone.

The human race is now entering upon a new phase of evolutionary progress, a phase in which, impelled by the forces of evolution itself, it must converge upon itself and convert itself into one single human organism dominated by a reconciliation of knowing and being in their inner unity and destined to make a qualitative leap into a higher form of consciousness that would transcend and complement individual consciousness as we know it, or otherwise destroy itself. For the entire universe is one vast field, potential for incarnation, and achieving incandescence here and there of reason and spirit. What to some is mystery and inscrutability, to others symbolizes and declares the very nature of the cosmic process. And in the whole world of *quality* with which category by the nature of our minds we necessarily make contact, we here and there apprehend pre-eminent value. This can be achieved only if we recognize that we are unable to focus our attention on the particulars of a whole without diminishing our comprehension of the whole, and of course conversely, we can focus on the whole only by diminishing our comprehension of the particulars which constitute the whole.

This Series is designed to present a kind of intellectual autobiography of each author, to portray the nature and meaning of the creative process for the creator and to show the relevance of his work to the feelings and aspirations of the man of flesh and bone. This Series endeavors to reflect also the influence of the work on the man and on society and to point to the freedom, or lack of freedom, to choose and pursue one profession rather than another.

It attempts to emphasize that the creator in any realm must surrender himself to a passionate pursuit of the hidden meaning of his labors, guided by deep personal intimations of an as yet undiscovered reality.

These volumes endeavor to indicate that it is impossible to know what constitutes a good society unless we know what defines a good individual. The self is determined by the values according to which it subordinates and integrates the rest of its values. If the values be transient, so is the self. If the values be dispersed and incoherent, so is the self. If they are organic and integrated, so is the self. The unity of human personality is its soundness. The unified self cannot be understood in terms of its constituent parts as dissected away from each other. So that finally what we see and what we do are no more and no less than what we are.

It is the effort of *The Credo Series* to define the new reality in which the estrangement of man and his work, resulting in the self-estrangement in man's existence, is overcome. This new reality is born through the reconciliation of what a man *knows* with what a man *is*. Being itself in all its presuppositions and implications can only be understood through the totality, through wholeness. St. Paul, who, like Isaiah before him, went into the market place not to secularize truth but to proclaim it, taught man that the "new creation" could be explained only by conquering the daemonic cleavages, the destructive split, in soul and cosmos. And that fragmentation always destroys a unity, produces a tearing away from the source and thereby creates disunity and isolation. The fruit can never be separated from the tree. The Tree of Life can never be disjoined from the Tree of Knowledge for both have *one and the same* root. And if man allows himself to fall into isolation, if he seeks to maintain a self segregated from the totality of which he is a necessary part, if he chooses to remain asunder, unrelated to the original context of all created things in which he too has his place—including his own labors—then this act of apostasy bears fruit in the demiurgical presumption of *magic*, a form of animism in which man seeks an authority of the self, placing himself above the law of the universe by attempting to separate the inseparable. He thus creates an unreal world of false contexts after having destroyed or deserted the real. And in this way the method of analysis, of scientific objectivity, which is good and necessary in its right place, is endowed with a destructive power when it is allowed to usurp a place for which it is not fitted.

The naturalist principle that man is the measure of all things has been shattered more than ever in our own age by the question, "What is the measure of man?" Postmodern man is more profoundly perplexed about the nature of man than his ancestors were. He is on the verge of spiritual and moral insanity. He does not know who he is. And having lost the sense of who and what he is, he fails to grasp the meaning of his fellow man, of his vocation, and of the nature and purpose of knowledge itself. For what is not understood cannot be known. And it is this cognitive faculty which is frequently abrogated by the "scientific" theory of knowledge, a theory that refuses to recognize the existence of comprehensive entities as distinct from their particulars. The central act of knowing is indeed that form of comprehension which is never absent from any process of knowing and is finally its ultimate sanction.

Science itself acknowledges as real a host of entities that cannot be described completely in materialistic or mechanistic terms, and it is this transcendence out of the domain of science into a region from which science itself can be appraised that *The Credo Series* hopes to expose. For the essence of the ebb and flow of experience, of sensations, the richness of the immediacy of directly apprehended knowledge, the metaphysical substance of what assails our being, is the very act itself of sensation and affection and therefore must escape the net of rational analysis, yet is intimately related to every cognitive act. It is this increasing intellectual climate that is calling into birth once more the compelling Socratic questions, "What is the purpose of life, the meaning of work?" "What is man?" Plato himself could give us only an indirect answer: "Man is declared to be that creature who is constantly in search of himself, a creature who at every moment of his existence must examine and scrutinize the conditions of his existence. He is a being in search of meaning."

Theory and life always go together. An organic conception of man and his work, man and society, man and the universe, is portrayed in First Corinthians 12 when Paul relates the famous story of the strife that once broke out between the parts of the human body. They refused to fulfill their special functions within the organism until they finally learned that they are all parts of one body and can exist and function only as such. For they all breathe together. And by so doing subordinate themselves to the presentation of the whole body. What may be an explanation of organic life in the human body may be transferred to the life in the universe and to the relationship between the interior and the exterior, for all is permeated by the life-giving creative power—by unity.

The authors in this endeavor are aware that man in the twentieth century finds himself in the greatest revolution since the discovery of agriculture. They show, each in his own way, that part of the meaning of our present turmoil may indeed lie in its being the means to reconcile thought and action, to overcome the parochialism of dogmas that only isolate man from man and man from the implicit meaning of his chosen profession. Our effort is to create an image of man intelligible and unitary, a microcosmic mirror of the greater macrocosm of which he is a part and in which he has his legitimate place in relation to the whole. For even the extraordinary successes of scientific predictions, the fruits of man's ingenuity in inventing the scientific method, seem comprehensible only on the basis that the human mind possesses an inherent logic closely parallel with the structure of the external world itself.

The very interdependence of the observer and the participant can no longer be ignored as part of the essential value of things. To take a definitive example from modern cosmology, it is challenging indeed to note that there is a most unusual connection between the existence of stars and the laws that govern the atomic nuclei. Emphasis is placed upon the existence, not the properties, of stars. For everyone expects the properties of stars and atomic nuclei to be related. It is the *connection* with the *existence* of stars that is so reassuring—and indeed surprising.

From this it is evident that there is present in the universe a *law* applicable to all nature including man and his work. Life itself then is seen to be a creative process elaborating and maintaining *order* out of the randomness of matter, endlessly generating new and unexpected structures and properties by building up associations that qualitatively transcend their constituent parts. This is not to diminish the importance of "scientific objectivity." It is, however, to say that the mind possesses a quality that cannot be isolated or known exclusively in the sense of objective knowledge. For it consists in that elusive humanity in us, our

self, that knows. It is that inarticulate awareness that in-
cludes and *comprehends* all we know. It consists in the
irreducible active voice of man and is recognized only in
other things, only when the circle of consciousness closes
around its universe of events.

The experience of the modern mind has been expressed
in terms of conflict produced by false dualisms, disruption,
self-destruction, meaninglessness, purposelessness and des-
peration. This character of our time has found its expression in literature, in art, in existential philosophy, in some
forms of natural science, in political demonologies, and is
explored in the psychology of the unconscious. Our authors
hope to indicate that through a quickening of awareness
man can overcome this dualism and can rise to face the
meaning of life and work, keeping his mind and energies
awake at full stretch. Such knowledge—that form of
knowledge which cannot be disjoined from being—will enable man to embrace life with passion and to work with
devotion. It will enable him to absorb experience with his
whole nature and thereby to fill a want that is satisfied
neither by action alone nor by thought alone. This unity of
being and *doing* has a justifiable claim to be called a form
of enchantment since through it men, who might otherwise
give in to the malice of circumstances and conditions, find
their old powers revived or new powers stirring within
them, and through these life is sustained, renewed and
fulfilled.

Man is now confronting himself with the compelling
need to create an organic identification between what he
is and what he *does*. For only in this way can the threat of
conformism and the treachery of abstraction, the plight of
the modern mind, be conquered. This split, inherited from
the seventeenth century, between the transitive and the in-
transitive, between the creator and the process of creativity,

has blunted man's appetite for experience. Language itself in our time has failed because man has forgotten that it is the mother of thought, because of its analytical emphasis and thus lacks ready means to convey associations, emotional or imaginative, that cluster around a subject and give to it a distinctive personal significance. In other words, the symbols by which man lives and has his being, that "tacit coefficient" * of articulate knowledge that is unanalyzable, now knocks at the portals of consciousness waiting to be admitted. For human nature loses its most precious quality when it is robbed of its sense of things beyond, unexplored and yet insistent.

The Credo Series belongs to those ideas that are intuitively conceived and that originate in spheres of a spiritual order and surprise thought, as it were, compelling it to transform its inherited notions conformably with its enlarged vision of the nature of things. It is as though the authors of the Series were recovering this reality out of a memory of a lost harmony, a memory latent in the soul and not distilled from the changing things of mere physical observation. In this way the inner unity of the known and the knower may be preserved, and the almost mythic intuition of reality thereby related to its conceptual and rational forms of expression. For man, unlike a machine, is an organism existing as an end in itself. He *is* the system on which causal explanations are based and to which they have to return; he *is* a historically existent whole, a four-dimensional entity, and not merely an abstraction from which statements about phenomena are deducible under the guise of eternity.

* See the classical work, *Personal Knowledge,* by Michael Polanyi for an enlarged meaning of the nature of reality. (Chicago University Press, 1958)

Our hope is to point to a new dimension of morality—not that of constraint and prohibition but a morality that lies as a fountainhead within the human soul, a morality of aspiration to spiritual experience. It suggests that necessity is laid upon us to infer entities that are not observed and are not observable. For an unseen universe is necessary to explain the seen. The flux is seen, but to account for its structure and its nature we infer particles of various kinds to serve as the vertices of the changing patterns, placing less emphasis on the isolated units and more on the structure and nature of relations. The process of knowing involves an immaterial becoming, an immaterial identification, and finally, knowledge itself is seen to be a dependent variable of immateriality. And somewhere along this spiritual pilgrimage man's pure observation is relinquished and gives way to the deeper experience of awe, for there can be no explanation of a phenomenon by searching for its origin but only by discerning its immanent law—this quality of transcendence that abides even in matter itself.

The present situation in the world and the vast accretion of knowledge have produced a serious anxiety, which may be overcome by re-evaluating the character, kinship, logic and operation of man in relation to his work. For work implies goals and intimately affects the person performing the work. Therefore the correlation and relatedness of ideas, facts and values that are in perpetual interplay could emerge from these volumes as they point to the inner synthesis and organic unity of man and his labors. For though no labor alone can enrich the person, no enrichment can be achieved without absorbing and intense labor. We then experience a unity of faith, labor and grace which prepares the mind for receiving a truth from sources over which it has no control. This is especially true since the great challenge of our age arises out of man's inventions in relation to his life.

Thus *The Credo Series* seeks to encourage the perfection not only of man's works but also and above all the fulfillment of himself as a person. And so we now are summoned to consider not only man in the process of development as a human subject but also his influence on the object of his investigation and creation. Observation alone is interference. The naïve view that we can observe any system and predict its behavior without altering it by the very act of observation was an unjustified extrapolation from Newton's *Celestial Mechanics*. We can observe the moon or even a satellite and predict its behavior without appreciably interfering with it, but we cannot do this with an amoeba, far less with a man and still less with a society of men. It is the heart of the question of the nature of work itself. If we regard our labors as a process of shaping or forming, then the fruits of our labors play the part of a mold by which we ourselves are shaped. And this means, in the preservation of the identity of the knower and the known, that cognition and generation, that is, creation, though in different spheres, are nevertheless alike.

It is hoped that the influence of such a Series may help to overcome the serious bifurcation of function and meaning and may show that the extraordinary crisis through which the world is passing can be fruitfully met by recognizing that knowledge has not been completely dehumanized and has not totally degenerated into a mere notebook over-crowded with formulas that few are able to understand or apply.

For mankind is now engaged in composing a new theme. Life refuses to be embalmed alive. Life cannot abjure life;

nothing that lives is born out of nothingness. But nothing, either, can preserve its form against the ceaseless flux of being. Life never manifests itself in negative terms. And our hope lies in drawing from every category of work a conviction that non-material values can be discovered in positive, affirmative, visible things. The estrangement between the temporal and non-temporal man is coming to an end, community is inviting communion and a vision of the human condition more worthy of man is engendered, connecting ever more closely the creative mind with the currents of spiritual energy which breaks for us the bonds of habit and keeps us in touch with the permanence of being in all its plenitude through our work.

And as, long ago, the Bearers of Bread were succeeded by the Bearers of Torches, so now, in the immediacies of life, it is the image of man and his vocation that can rekindle the high passion of humanity in its quest for light. Refusing to divorce work from life or love from knowledge, it is action, it is passion that enhances our being.

We live in an expanding universe and also in the moral infinite of that other universe, the universe of man. And along the whole stretched arc of this universe we may see that extreme limit of complicity where reality seems to shape itself within the work man has chosen for his realization. Work then becomes not only a way of knowledge, it becomes even more a way of life—of life in its totality. For the last end of every maker is himself.

"And the places that have been desolate for ages shall be built in thee: thou shalt raise up the foundations of generation and generation; and thou shalt be called the repairer of the fences, turning the paths into rest." *

—RUTH NANDA ANSHEN

* Isaiah, 58:12

THE CHALLENGE OF THE PASSING YEARS:

My Encounter with Time

PREFACE

This book is concerned with the questions that our passage through time sets for us all. Time affects us in so many ways. We use it; we abuse it; we enjoy it; we fear it. It is a datum of all our decisions. It seals our mortality, ending alike our troubles and our joys. It is the condition and the limit of all we have, our opportunities, the gifts of nature, the ups and downs of fortune.

The way we respond to the challenges of time is a test of what we are, of what we are becoming. We grow older day by day, older in the calendar. Does that fact disturb us greatly, little, sometimes, often? How else are we growing in the same time? How much of our time do we enjoy, doing what? Do we frequently or seldom feel that the time was really well spent? The answers we would give to these questions reveal our philosophy of time. We all acquire one, though we rarely, if ever, venture to spell it out.

I offer my particular philosophy, my credo *concerning time, in the pages that follow. In doing so I try also to convey some ideas about the relation between time and some other big realities. Often we speak misleadingly about these things. The first chapter deals with the most common of all our misunderstandings. Time teases our minds when we try to think about it, but there is a reward in trying.*

My credo *exalts, in the first place, a form of freedom*

on which our modern civilization bears down hard. It is
not one of the freedoms whose praises men sing. It is not
celebrated like, say, the four freedoms. But it holds one
of the keys to the good life. It is essential for all creative
effort, and without it there is little satisfaction in work
or in play. Let us call it freedom under time. We imply
the need for it when we complain that time is a task-
master, that it waits for no man, that it drives us faster
than we want to go.

Time as measured is the enemy of time as lived; in this
proposition I try to express the problem of the achievement of this freedom. There are various ways in which
we become the bondsmen of time. The most obvious is
when the work we do is denuded of interest for us, say
as schoolboys squirming for the closing bell; or office
workers whose thoughts are on the evening's sport; or
machine tenders listlessly pursuing a prescribed routine;
or lawyers preparing a brief for a case that leaves them
cold. Another type of situation occurs when under pressure we allot to a significant task a period too short to
permit us to do justice to it—or to ourselves—so that we
pluck the unripe fruit from the tree. Few of us are lucky
enough to be entirely free from these pressures, but by
taking thought we can still save ourselves from much of
the fret and the erosion of the servitude to measured time.

The body has its own tempo, and so has the mind. By
defending these tempos against gross violations we guard
our integrity. So may we learn to make work more congenial and leisure and the companionship of our fellows
a more refreshing and more stimulating experience. So
may we learn the more fully to live our time and thus to
be at one with ourselves.

PART ONE

Preliminary Notions About Time

I

THE TIME DIMENSION

Time goes, you say? Ah no!
Alas, Time stays, we go.
— HENRY AUSTIN DOBSON,
The Paradox of Time

WHAT DOES time mean? What does time mean to you and me? The two questions are really very different. The second we can in some measure answer: it is the question that will mainly concern us in this book. The first puzzles us the more we try to think about it, and we end with little more than a question mark. In what sense does time *exist?* Time dates all beginnings and endings; can time itself have a beginning or an end? Can we think of it as a dimension; but it seems so different, so elusive compared with our familiar three dimensions?

From these complexities we turn with a kind of relief to our common-sense notion of time, time as it is experienced. But even here we cannot wholly escape our prior question. Our common-sense ideas may be misleading here, as so often elsewhere.

1

Usually, for example, we think of time as passing, always passing, all too swiftly passing. Our lives are brief episodes in the chain of generations. Time was passing thus ages before we were born and will continue to pass through countless generations yet to be. After endless ages the plenitude of unpassed time will be as great as before. A tiny unit of this plenitude is allotted to us. What concerns us is the way our measure of time runs out, so many years ticked off inexorably, day after day.

Time, we say, is moving by. It is an ever flowing stream, not one that carries us with it but one that leaves us behind. But let us pause over this common way of speaking. Is it time that passes or flows or moves at all? We cannot *feel* its flow. It is not like the flow of a stream, whose motion we actually perceive. We look at the motion of the second hand of a watch as it courses over the dial. What we observe is motion through space, the graduated motion of a mechanism that registers for us equal intervals of time as the hand passes over equal areas of a circumference. What we observe is movement through space; what we infer, without warrant as we shall presently see, is that movement *through* space is a measure of the movement *of* time. What we are aware of is a time interval, not a time movement. During this interval we perceive change taking place, change around us and change in ourselves.

Where there is change, there is before and after. The interval is time. Time is the dimension of the universe that allows change to happen.

It is always the fact of change, change of some sort, that makes us conscious of time. And most of all it is the fact of change in ourselves. We are other than we have been. What we sense is not time itself but the lapse of time. What we are aware of is not the work of time but the changes that take place within the time interval.

What makes time so significant to us is that the changes

that occur over periods of time are often successive steps or stages in a process, a process over which we usually have little or no control, although it may greatly concern us. We apprehend time from the observation of succession or process, but time itself is indifferent to the processes that occur in it. We know time only as that universal continuum in or along or through which change and duration, beginnings and endings, and not least the happenings of our own lives, occur. This universal continuum, the unimaginable principle or dimension we call time, is punctuated, recognized, filled and measured by the processes that take place in it. Like the atom or its particles time cannot be imaged, cannot be given any kind of substantiveness by the human mind.

Time is a principle of order. It makes room for and puts limits on the endless procession of created or composite things. Every system, every structure, every constituted object the universe holds is dated. Life appeared on earth so many million years ago. The earth is hundreds of millions of years old. The sun and the whole vast galaxy of which it is a unit are so many billions of years old. Physicists talk of the age of the entire universe of countless galaxies spread through the inconceivable immensity of space. Everything is older or younger, whether the reckoning is in seconds or in light-years. Everything is moving under law to some predeterminate end. Everything had a beginning—except the timeless, the uncomposite, the uncreated.

When we say that time sets its limit to things, we do not mean that time is a lawgiver. We speak of the ravage of time. We say time's hand cannot be stayed. We picture time as carrying a scythe that mows all things down. All this again is a manner of speech, sometimes, indeed, a way of thinking. But once more we should remember that time should not be thought of as a force. Time as such creates nothing, destroys nothing. The rocks are worn down, and stars grow old, empires decay and men pass from childhood to age—not because time works on them but because energies within them and around them, as they wax and wane, conspire to that effect. The wheel, once set in motion, would turn, and the top would spin forever, if no forces impinged on them. The whole of existence is meshed within the eternal action and reaction of the energy systems that build and change and weaken and destroy all created things.

We know time then as a dimension, a co-ordinate of the universe. To put it in the roughest terms, space is the dimension in which things exist, and time is the dimension in which things change. Whatever other role time may play in the grand scheme of nature, it has always one specific operation: it makes change possible. Without change, without process, we could not even know of time.

All created things exist as processes in time, even when they seem unchanging. Process means continuous change. Even the most enduring of things is changing imperceptibly every moment, though it may be years or centuries or ages before the change is manifest. All things exist as bundles of energies subject to the impact of environmental energies. They cannot but change continuously. Only the uncreated can be beyond the conjunctures of time and change, beyond the destiny of beginning and end.

Time itself, being a dimension along which everything moves, cannot be thought of as being slowed or hastened. Time has no *pace* whatever. It is only process that has pace and that can be manipulated so as to go slower or faster. Such manipulation plays a major role in the arts, crafts and techniques of every civilization. We "save time" only in the sense that we control the pace of processes. We "arrest time" only in the sense that we delay the initiation of processes. The seed can be preserved

and made to sprout at a later time. Recently a refined
process for the dry freezing of sperm has made it possible to delay fertilization for months and even years, and
theoretically it might be delayed for centuries. Thus even
the time of living may be postponed, as though time itself were arrested. But that is a figurative way of speaking.
Time, the condition of change, is forever itself unchanged,
a pure contentless dimension along which change occurs.

Time, like space, is equally remote from any descriptive
qualification, equally a form within which, or a condition
under which, all existences have position, scale, reality.

Such statements, however, point merely to a superficial
resemblance between these two universal aspects of a
single cosmos, each of which poses to the scientific theorist
profound problems of interpretation that lie beyond the
pretensions of this inquiry. What we shall mostly be concerned with is the role of time on the human plane; the
way men conceive of it and the way they respond to the
inexorable limits of their own brief span of it; the expedients they contrive to relieve or evade the pressures
and problems of their arclike course through it; and the
doctrines and surmises they entertain concerning time and
the human condition.

II
TIME AND CHANGE

There are no footprints pointing backward.
—HORACE, *Epistles*

LET US look at what might appear at first sight a signal distinction between time and that other cosmic co-ordinate, space. All created things exist in time and space. They all move in space or through space, and they all move in time or through time. They change continuously their locus in space. Continuously they change their locus in time. It would seem so far that time and space are primary immobiles where all else is process, process through space, process through time. But there seems a difference, for human life a poignant difference. An object can move from one place to another and back, in effect, to where it was before. A person can travel and return. But nothing created, nothing animate or inanimate, can go back in time to where—or to what—it was before. One might say, the traveler returns to his starting point, but the place from which he started has itself, if imperceptibly, changed while he was away. And we might answer, yes, but he returns to the place he left and finds it again as it would have been had he never traveled. But there is no return whatever through time. It is the common thought that has been given somberly beautiful expression in an ode by Catullus to his loved Lesbia, which we may translate as follows:

6

> The sun can set and rise on high,
> But we, when once our little light
> Has set, must then together lie
> Sleeping in everlasting night.

The clock can be turned back but not the time the clock has measured. The motion picture can be re-run, but the seal of time is on the doings it records.

Once more, this is a way of thinking, a way of representing the relentlessness of the has-been, the lengthening record of the past that leaves its inerasable imprint on the present. We speak of time as invincible; we picture it as carrying a scythe:

> And nothing stands but for his scythe to mow.

But, again it is not time that makes or that destroys. The moving finger that writes and, having writ, moves on is not the finger of time but the finger of power, of the creative and destructive forces that work in and on all created things.

Time does not move on. The endless flux is the flux within the constructs, the organizations, the unities, the beings that emerge from the temporary conjunctures of a dynamic universe. Since they are all composite, they are subject to the timeless energies that pervade the universe. The equilibrium they preserve, the cohesion they maintain, the lives they cherish are dated from the first. Dissolution is inherent in their beings. They are all in process, upbuilding or downgrading. Time and space remain eternally omnipresent, conditioning but also making possible all created things. Time itself is not in process, but all process is in time and space. Space is not mobile, but all mobility is in space and time. Time does not pass; the passage is ours through time.

What then remains of the inveterate notion that time is a one-way road, moving from the irremediable past into an ever-passing present that dies every instant it is born?

Let us turn again to the analogy of space. We go back and forth repeatedly over the same traveled ground. The sun rises every morning and sets every evening. But we too rise in the morning and retire at night. We are repeating a time sequence just as we repeat a space sequence when we travel back and forth to and from our place of work. Shall we say, yes, but we cannot go back to yesterday morning. Do we then go back over yesterday's road to yesterday's office and return to yesterday's home? Perhaps we see no difference in the road or in the office or in the physical home. But they are different just as we are different. The processes of change they undergo may have different time scales than the processes of our mortal lives. What we have traveled over is not space but material objects. They change, and we change. Time and space are beyond all processes. No motion can be attributed to them. In ways beyond our understanding, time and space together provide the eternal cosmic environment within which the field forces of the universe range, within which the objects thus created fulfill the course of their existence.

When we say time moves on and only onward, we are concerned that the ravages of time cannot be reversed. Youth's a stuff that will not endure. Some processes are in all significant respects repeatable; others are dated once and for all. The organism has, in broad terms, a one-direction course from birth to death, though there are ways in which the span may be somewhat enlarged. We are concerned also because we ourselves are agents in a world of change, and a deed once done entails consequences that may well be irreparable. In this sense we understand the strong saying of a Greek tragic poet that "even God cannot make unbegotten the things that have been done."

All process occupies an area of time just as it occupies an area of space. Time is a continuum that stretches infinitely in every direction, just as space is a continuum somehow cognate with time. All events exist somewhere in time in just the same sense in which all objects exist somewhere in space. As organic beings we are somewhere in time just as we are somewhere in space. The light of consciousness at each particular moment of time is aware of a particular spot of space. Beyond these immediate particulars, it reviews with the aid of memory a thought-linked scheme of events and situations, so that the present becomes part of a continuous and more or less coherent process. Within this scheme each immediate present passes imperceptibly into the next.

The brief sketch here presented of the relation of time and change ignores some deep-lying questions over which philosophers have disputed without contributing much, if any, enlightenment. The simple fact is that we cannot comprehend the reality of time and space. We cannot, for example, conceive of time as ever ending—so we must think of it as infinite. But that conception is in turn quite baffling. So with our presumptive infinitude of space. How can space ever end? The riddle is beyond us. We cannot imagine space any more than we can perceive it. Nor can we feel the time we pass through or imagine what *through* means. We must posit time because we do experience and do perceive change, and time is the roominess change must have. We must posit space because we perceive objects that occupy it and because we and they travel through something we call space. The existence of time and space are our primal postulates, because they are necessary for any comprehension of the world around us and because the business of living must always and inevitably take them into account.

III

PAST, PRESENT AND FUTURE

> *All things does long unnumbered time bring*
> *forth from darkness and bury from the light.*
> —SOPHOCLES, *Ajax*

As CONSCIOUS BEINGS we live *in* the now, in each new emergent now. We have lived *through* the past, and we expect to live *into* the future. Only in the present do we think and do; only in the present can things happen to us. The present is the time of experiencing. We cannot feel past pains or enjoy future pleasures—though the memory of past pains may affect our present feelings, and the anticipation of future pleasures may give us some present enjoyment.

The present, then, is the time of decision, the time of opportunity, while the moving finger writes. The present is both the time of living and the time of preparation for future living. All this may seem very obvious, but as always with the elusive fact of time, some deep questions are hidden beneath its obviousness.

The present in which we act and think is not a tick of the clock, not a flash of light that disappears on the instant into the memoried past. If we want to appreciate the relation between the present and the future, the present and the past, we must first of all understand that the present, our present, is not like a point on a line, the ever lengthening line on which we move from the past

into the future. We do not act, we do not think, in a succession of split seconds. The mood we are in, the pleasure or pain we feel right now, occupies an appreciable
present time. The present is for conscious beings a period,
not an infinitesimal break between an infinite past and an
infinite future.

We said "for conscious beings." What meaning then has
the present for material objects, for inanimate nature?
What is the now for a mountain, a piece of metal or a
star? These objects do not act or feel, do not look back
on their past or plan their future. Obviously the present
has not the significance for inanimate objects, even for
vegetative objects, that it has for the conscious being. If
by any chance we should ascribe to them a meaningful
present, it is only because they are observed or thought of
in relation to our own conscious present. They are all at
some stage of the particular process of change to which
they are respectively subject. Process is continuous, no
matter how slow it may appear. There is no cessation, no
staying, of the internal changes material objects undergo
or of the impact on them of environmental forces. The
now in which we observe them is merely one of the innumerable nows through which they pass, if they endure
any length of time. The now of process is every successive
phase of exposure to change.

The exposure scale is theoretically divisible into infinitesimal units. Modern physics has discovered subatomic particles that have a life of around 10^{-20} seconds
—which means one second divided by one followed by
twenty zeros, a quantity hopelessly beyond any conception. Yet even in this inconceivably short time they, too,
are undergoing a process. What is the now for such a
particle? What is the now for any physical object? If process is continuous, its hypothetical now is instantaneous
beyond any micrometer's range.

The position we have just presented respecting the in-

finitesimal present tense of the whole physical world leads
to a curious impasse. Since nothing can happen except in
the present, and since whatever happens in the future depends on what happens in the present, the whole tremendous universe with its ceaseless ongoing processes, without
beginning and without end, hangs on the happenings of the
infinitely thin line that divides the future from the past.
This line is so thin that the conclusion staggers the imagination. We spoke of a particle that exists for 10^{-20} seconds, but even that minuteness is itself theoretically divisible to the nth degree. Since the past is no more and the
future is not yet, must we conclude that the universe is
actual only when it is in one or another of these incredible
fractions of time?

Present-day science, as we shall explain near the close
of this book, shows a way out of this impasse. While abstract mathematical time is infinitely divisible, process need
not be thought of in the same way. It may have its own
quanta, which are the units of change. Moreover, the new
Einsteinian doctrine of time and space rejects the notion
that the universe moves by separate tiny moments of time
out of the past into the present and through the future.

For the conscious being the answer is certainly clear
enough. For him the present is no mere instant but a
bracket of varying amplitude and duration. At this moment, in this moment, you are reading. You are not
reading single words. You are reading clauses and sen-
tences. Your attention is directed to meanings that are
conveyed in a structure of words. You hold a meaning
before you, a meaning that took a number of words, a
number also of seconds on the watch, before it appeared.
The whole of that meaning enters into your present consciousness, and it itself is only an aspect of a more
inclusive meaning all of which, presumably, is apprehended
by you as you read on. The present "moment" is then, for

you, not a mere instant of time but a sizable period longer or shorter according to the range of the bracket.

A comparison of the now of time with the here of space may serve at this point. While you read these words you have a book in front of you, and your attention is directed to a particular page and a particular part of the page. But you see the book and are aware of a background. If a change suddenly took place in the nearer background you would at once notice it. Your here is, say, a chair in a room, and in the periphery of your vision there may be a strip of wall on which a picture hangs. At the same time you are aware of being in a room that is in a certain building in a certain city. If noise broke in on your reading, you would immediately locate it as being in the building or, say, outside in the street. In short, your conscious here has a focus of awareness that is surrounded by a hinterland dimming out who knows how far.

Just as the conscious now is not a point in time but a time bracket, so the conscious here is not a point in space, not position without magnitude, but an area held for an appreciable time in the span of consciousness. There is the focus of interest, the corona of recognition reaching to the margin of direct perception, and beyond that a penumbra of consciousness, the vaguer sentience of what lies beyond.

The here, as seen, heard, felt or however sensed or recognized, is text and context of the conscious moment. In reflective moods some past here, some there and then, may be summoned into recollection to constitute a major part of the moment's filling. Indeed, in more abstract cogitation the sensed here may be no more than marginal to consciousness, while the focus of attention is an idea, say a problem or an issue.

As the words emerge into light on a moving newscast, so the conscious now emerges in full continuity with the passing and past nows. While life lasts, the stream of consciousness moves on, unbroken even when it enters the tunnel of sleep. In the underground passage the subconscious here, the dream here, is detached from the waking here and consists mainly of snatches of recollected theres. The waking memory recalls at best only glimpses of sleep-time experience, but the evidence strongly suggests that the light of the conscious now is only dimmed, dimmed below the memory threshold but not extinguished during sleep.

Each conscious now is not like a link in a chain of separate nows. No now begins as a whole or ends as a whole. Every now subtly becomes a newer now as the past closes in on the older. The stream of consciousness moves from and into time, broader or narrower, deeper or shallower, according to the capacity for living. It has deeper currents where its light is shadowy and depths which are sensed dimly or not at all but which may in any moment upsurge into the area of clear light.

But the metaphor of the stream does little justice to the marvelous way in which the ever-moving conscious present weaves new experience into the unity of perception and of thought-mode it inherits continuously from its past. It is the life itself that moves into and through its renewed moments of being, the same life that has lived and lives on into its own future, adapting new to old experiences, registering impressions, subtly changing its continuous identity as it seeks a fulfillment never to be wholly attained. For life is—or has—this unique energy possessed of sensitivity and perceptiveness that makes for itself a web of relationships, thus binding its past to its future.

Thus, too, the present becomes, within the area of conscious behavior, doubly determinative of the future. There is here not only the universal law-bound process that carries all things, inorganic or organic, continuously from the past to the future; there is also the cultural heritage of the conscious being who can look before and after, thus enlarging and supplementing the existential bracket of the present as he endeavors to build his own road into the future. However precarious and short the road he designs, however much at the mercy of disruptive forces unforeseen or unforeseeable, it nevertheless changes, within its area, the aspect of things to come. The physical as well as the cultural environment of man has already been considerably altered because of his designing mind, though often enough the accomplishment turns out to be rather different from the design. What human beings have in the past built for today endures into tomorrow, and what they build for tomorrow will change a further tomorrow.

Thus the distinctive nature of the conscious present confers a new significance on the past and links it in a new way to the future.

IV

TIME AND THE TIMELESS

> *Then gin I think on that which Nature sayd,*
> *Of that same time when no more Change shall*
> *be,*
> *But stedfast rest of all things firmly stayd*
> *Upon the pillars of Eternity*
> *That is contrayr to mutability.*
> —EDMUND SPENSER, *The Faerie Queene*

CHANGE is insistent in all our experience, change in ourselves, change in our condition and in our relationships. Man's own unrestingness is tuned to a changing society and a changing environment. But ever and again he yearns for a change from change; he tires of a restlessness that always turns upon itself. At times the feeling of an encroaching timeless reality breaks in on his unfulfilled strivings. It may be in the form of religious intimations of an eternity in the thought of which these strivings are vain or irrelevant, or it may be in the presence of death and the sense of its final peace. Then the timeless looms both as a threat and as a release.

The vision of the philosopher and of the poet as well as that of the theologian has been engrossed with the thought of a timeless reality. The philosophic expression of it was first notably presented by Plato, who found his timeless realities in the generic patterns of forms, the principles or archetypes, of which all particular objects are temporary embodiments. There are, for example, men and dogs and trees and tables. They are all short-lived, but then there are always more men and dogs and trees and tables. The individuals pass, but the form, the type, endures. Through all the generations of men, man, the principle or form of manness, persists. It belongs to the abiding reality. And so with all things animate or inanimate. The visible, tangible representations fleetingly take on the shapes of the timeless.

In a famous passage of his *Republic,* Plato resorted to the parable or myth of the cave. In the world of the senses we live among the shadows, the mere simulacra of the timeless realities. We are like prisoners in a cave, chained so that we see only the shadows cast upon its wall by the real objects as they pass by in the sunlight outside the mouth of the cave. Knowing no better, we think the shadows are the real things. But the realities belong to the upper world; they are perceived not by the senses but by the mind. They belong not to the lower world of the senses but to the upper world where the light of reason shines. A cognate conception, though less picturesquely expressed, underlies the whole range of "idealistic" philosophy up to the present day.

There is, however, an indisputable category of timeless realities that can be adduced without resort to the philosopher, a category amply sufficient to provide the contrast between the creatures of change and the firmament of the changeless. In this context we shall mean by timeless realities any existences that are not subject to processes of change or, alternatively, that change only in the sense that they may assume and resume any one of two or more reversible forms.

We distinguish three broad divisions within this category, as follows:

1. *Dimensional Ultimates.* Here we set down time and space, within which every existence has its limits and its

particular dimensional properties. We think nowadays of a four-dimensional scheme of things, space providing three dimensions and time the fourth. If there are other dimensions than these, they lie beyond our power of conception. It may seem curious to include time itself in the category of the timeless, but when we properly think of time not as something that is moving on but as something through which all existence moves, we can see that it is timeless in the same sense in which space is.

2. *Uncompounded Physical Entities.* We refer here to the irreducible entities that in their combinations and relationships make up the contents of the physical universe. They fall into two main classes which we provisionally distinguish as follows:

a. *Atomic Corpuscles.* The constitutents of the atom. Originally the atom itself was regarded as the ultimate constituent of all material things. Modern physics, having first discovered the atom, went on to the discovery that these infinitesimal units were still not ultimate but were composed of corpuscles, such as electrons and protons and neutrons and a variety of others, a complex and still unexplored array that makes the constitution of matter a greater riddle than ever before. Many of these particles have their antiparticles with opposite electric signs. A few of them, like the neutrino, are totally weightless— another revolutionary concept. Many of them can change into others in accordance with a determinate pattern. How then can we include them in the category of the changeless? So far as we know, they do not go through *processes* of change but merely transformation. And some of them, like the electron, appear to be immutable in any sense. Perhaps we can also say they are all potentially there "from the beginning" and will be "to the end of time." They are the constituents of the universe, forming atoms and molecules and stars.

b. *Primal Energies.* The fundamental forces that bind

the atom; the forces that by their attractions and repulsions determine the relationships of all material things great and small; the forces that radiate throughout the universe. Included here are electromagnetic, gravitational, thermo-dynamic and mechanical energies and the various kinds of radiant energy.

The two classes we have here distinguished may in the last resort be only one. The famous Einstein equation of mass and energy ($E=MC^2$) has broken down our distinction, and the discovery that radiant energy consists of high-velocity particles of various kinds supports the conclusion that we are here in the presence of a single unitary type of fundamental cosmic entity. In the great ocean of mutability one eternal constant is the sum of energy and mass. We are here discounting one modern theory which holds that new matter in the form of hydrogen atoms is being created—out of nothing.

3. *Cosmic Laws.* The underlying laws by which all things are always bound, laws inherent in the very nature of the cosmos. The laws of motion, the equation of mass and energy, the conservation of charge, the quantum prin-ciple are examples, though the manner in which we state these laws may be inadequate and far from final.

In any event these unchanging laws—and should we not include the mathematical principles inherent in their operation?—constitute the firmament of the universe, the assurance of a steadfast order, strictly a cosmos, although all created or constructed objects or systems of objects are ceaselessly changing. This order abides, untouched by its passage through time. All constancy and all change be-come then the expression of changeless, ever-ruling law.

Throughout this discussion we have spoken of the time-less rather than of the eternal. Are the two attributions not then identical? Some distinction, we hold, may prop-erly be made between them. We identified the timeless with the changeless. The universe itself, the whole inconceivable ambit of existence, cannot be thought of as having a beginning or an end. When some physicists speak of the universe as having had a beginning at some point of time billions of years away, they are thinking of *our* kind of universe. If, for example, they conjecture it came through a tremendous explosion of some all-containing, undifferentiated gas when it reached a high degree of compression, the "matter" that thereafter differentiated into stars and planets and atomic elements and all the rest must have been there before the "beginning," and in the endless reaches of preceding time must have had many another opportunity to differentiate. No imagination is powerful enough to conjecture an *absolute* beginning of the universe. The universe then, in this broader sense, must be thought of as both eternal and changeful.

The traditional conception of God is one that attributes eternity rather than timelessness. This indeed is inevitable for any conception of an immortal being, since any such being must be regarded as active, even if only in the process of contemplation, and therefore as doing different things at different times. A certain inconsistency is present here. Thus God is said to be "the same yesterday, today and forever"; in Him "is no variableness, neither shadow nor turning." But at the same time He is spoken of as forgiving and showing mercy and answering prayer and so forth—all attributes that imply a change of attitude. The inconsistency is irremediable, since all such conceptions are at best only echoes of meanings we cannot reach.

PART TWO

Modes of Existence
Through Time

V

THE FORMS OF CONSTANCY
AND CHANGE

> *Worlds on worlds are rolling ever*
> *From creation to decay.*
> —PERCY BYSSHE SHELLEY

ALL THINGS, other than the primary infinitesimals, are always changing, but since the change is swift or slow, obvious or hidden, drastic or minor, we think of some as enduring, others as transient. We speak of the everlasting hills, but in the course of ages they sink and rise. We speak of the eternal stars, but though they last billions of years, they too are in process. They have their beginnings and their endings; they expand and shrink; they are younger or older, intensely bright or descending toward darkness. Endurance or transience is relative to our viewpoint and above all to our own little span.

Some things we think of as continuing rather than as

21

enduring, because while they undergo significant change, they still retain some characteristic aspects or structure. We think of the system as continuing because the form endures through change or because some distinctive feature endures. The fossils of trilobites are discovered in formations many millions of years old—the form endures for ages though the creature was quite short-lived. Or again a process of change may exhibit a particular trend or pattern, and there again we find continuity, but the continuity of a changing form. There is continuity everywhere, since all things undergo processes. It ranges from the most imperceptibly graded change of substance or of form to the mere linkage of a chain or the juxtaposition of beads strung on a thread. An illustration of continuity without total change of substance is offered in the old dilemma of the logicians about the pair of originally silk stockings so often darned with wool that they had become all-wool. The logicians asked the unanswerable question whether they were still the same pair of stockings.

Of all the kinds of continuity the most remarkable is evolution—evolution in its fuller sense, in which it seems applicable only to organic being. Here the basis of continuity is the germ plasm by means of which the organism is reproduced. But it is reproduced with a most significant difference. The variations and mutations of the reproductive intermixture of genes ramify in the course of ages into the families and orders and genera and species of the vast biological realm and in the process bring forth higher types, the process that thus far has led from minute specks of virus-like cells up to Homo sapiens.

Associated with continuity, we have also the indirect bond of succession. In a succession the unit items are discontinuous, though back of them there persists either an enduring pattern or form or the continuity of a system of some kind. Take, for example, the strata of a geological formation as they are successively laid down in the course of ages, such as the Pleistocene, the Pliocene, the Miocene and so forth. We catalogue in like manner the successive appearances of plant types and animal types, the various historical epochs and periods, the successively prevalent types of expression in the different arts. But the list has no end, for the successive ticks of the clock punctuate the mostly invisible modifications of all created things.

The successive items in a series may come immediately after one another, or they may follow at longer or shorter intervals as, say, a series of windfalls or disasters, wet years or dry, good harvests or bad harvests. We are frequently running into successions of this sort, whether we attribute them to luck or to fate or to providence. We seem, perhaps, particularly prone to regard evils as coming in series. "When troubles come, they come not single spies but in battalions."

Certain types of succession have taken strong hold of the imagination. One that has had considerable impact on economic doctrines and on philosophies of history is the cyclical pattern, regarded as the repetition of a succession that regularly returns to its starting point, in other words, fulfills a cycle or circle. Nature is prolific in series of this kind—the cycle of the seasons through spring, summer, autumn and winter, back to spring again. So with the phases of the moon or the annual wheeling of the constellations so that, for example, the plow turns by degrees "upside down" and then gradually assumes its original position. The stages of life are regarded as forming a similar series, from the spring of early youth to the winter of old age. But here the cycle renews itself not through winter passing into spring again, but in the successive generations. The analogy is applied to the ups and downs of economic prosperity and depression, and some economists have exercised much ingenuity in attempting to show that this cycle repeats itself at regular intervals of so many years; but indeed it takes much ingenuity to make out a plausible case here. Again, some historians and philosophers of history see civilizations, empires and nations as following, and always destined to follow, a similar course of rise, flowering, decline and fall. And in ancient days there was cherished the belief that once upon a time a golden age began on earth, attained its crown and disappeared until in the fullness of time the world's great age would begin anew.

Whether in the tangled skein of human affairs there can be found any series that corresponds to the ever-renewed cyclical course of various natural processes remains a dubious proposition. The tendency to discover similarly regulated patterns in the life histories of peoples and empires may be due less to the adequate testimony of the evidences than to the wishful attempt to impose a neat pattern on the untidiness of history. Certainly civilizations and empires and social movements and cultural achievements flourish and then suffer some decline or transformation. But if history repeats itself, it is always with disconcerting differences. The complex array of incessantly changing conditions and the responses to them of variously motivated authorities and groups make every situation distinctive. Only one Caesar crosses the Rubicon, and only once did the wrecks of the Armada strew the shore of Ireland. Various broad types of situations do frequently succeed one another in a certain order, such as the process from oligarchy to democracy and from democracy to Caesarism. But the clock of history never, it would seem, turns back to where it was before.

This reflection brings us to our fourth category, recurrence. Recurrence is simply the reappearance of a phenomenon or situation with no necessary presumption of a causal connection. Possibly the particular conjuncture of conditions that explained the first appearance may have again occurred to occasion the later one, or on the other hand a different conjuncture may have somehow evoked a phenomenon similar to the former one. Recurrence may take place after a short or long interval. It may come unheralded, like a new visitation of an epidemic. Or it may be the more or less predictable outcome of a given situation, like a second riot in a badly managed prison. Or it may be the manifestation of one stage in a cyclical process, the other stages of which are beyond our powers of observation, like the return of a meteor.

These four modes of existence through time—duration, continuity, succession and recurrence—take on, as we shall see in the next chapter, a special and quite distinctive quality in our human experience. There are characteristic types of duration, continuity, succession and recurrence that are the very creatures of our consciousness and that together constitute our essential experience of time.

VI

THE CONSCIOUSNESS OF
CONSTANCY AND CHANGE

> *Time's wheel runs back or stops; potter and clay endure.*
>
> —ROBERT BROWNING, *Rabbi Ben Ezra*

In the light of our experience the four modes of existence through time take on quality as well as quantity. We begin with the quality of conscious duration.

In the realm of consciousness as in that of the physical world process is continuous, but the embrace of the mind holds its now as a duration in which it perceives external objects and feels and thinks. Each now passes so undistinguishably into the then and admits so smoothly the oncoming now that it is impossible to say how long any conscious now endures.

What makes the transition even more indiscernible is that the *content* of consciousness, the focus of interest, is often stable through many successive nows. The same concern, the same problem, may engross attention without a break for a considerable length of time. It will of course have various aspects, one or another assuming more prominence in the process while nevertheless the complex of aspects remains within the ambit of consciousness. Likewise a strong emotion, dominated, say, by love or hate, by a prospect or a peril, may drive out for a spell all other considerations. And even when we turn again to some work in hand, the emotion insists on breaking in. It creates a feeling-tone that colors all our doing, whether the tone be bright or somber.

There are practices of contemplation, usually religious or philosophical in design, in which the disciple is trained to reflect steadfastly on a single object of devotion or a single idea to the exclusion of all other thoughts. Both Buddhism and some forms of Christianity encourage total absorption in this kind of contemplation.

It is a hard discipline, and for the less strong-minded and the less single-minded adherents the attitude of fixed contemplation sometimes conceals the intrusion of alien or even outrageously unbecoming thoughts.

Where, however, the goal is finally achieved, not merely by the exercise of will power but with entire emotional commitment, we reach that total identification of the subject with the undeviating object of its interest that Henri Bergson called "pure duration." We have all on occasion found ourselves wholly engrossed in some quest or some problem that in effect fascinated us, so that our interest in it excluded all other preoccupations. When this interest is one that not only concerns us deeply—when, for example, it is not some overwhelming danger or urgent necessity—but is a cause to which we are dedicated or a relationship that enlists the service of our whole personality, we become oblivious of time for a spell. The past is fused in the present, embraced within it, a present so completely energized that it rides freely with the onward flow of consciousness.

When we are wholly engrossed in any such manner, we are forgetful of time. And when some interruption does occur, when some other demand becomes so insistent that we must attend to it, we are likely to be surprised that so many hours have gone by. While the spell lasted, it was as though we were living out of time. And we look back with a feeling of genuine satisfaction. We have not lived *through* the time; we have lived it.

Such engrossment, however complete it seems, cannot be thought of as sheer or pure duration. It is rather a continuity wholly dominated by an emotionally charged content. We speak of the stream of consciousness, and there are times when it is so still that it seems to be motionless, while at other times it is more like a tumultuous torrent with endless variations in between. But the continuity that is life is too subtle and too multiform to be pinned down by any metaphor.

There are other aspects of the continuity of consciousness that wholly mark it off from any physical continuity. One is that it descends, as it were, into a tunnel for a period every day, the tunnel of sleep. It is muted but still in motion, to emerge with new impetus and resume its more active course.

Another aspect is the greater range of the continuity of consciousness, not only in breadth but also in depth. In the physical realm all change is presumed to be the direct result of the conditions present and operative in the occurrence of the change. But consciousness, especially in its higher levels, has processes of communication not only with the passing moment but also with the upsurging memories of its past experience. Thus does its past inform and enrich and selectively stimulate its present.

A similar bond of continuity, based on this recall of the past, unites the members of every group. Human groups accumulate traditions, mores, lores, modes of thought. This whole cultural complex, this legacy from the layers of the past, is not all at any time equally alive in the mental background of behavior. Some of it is overlaid, seemingly forgotten, superseded. Different groups in the society are very unequally responsive to it on different occasions. But some new development or some crisis may evoke a movement to revive old doctrines or old cultural attitudes or old styles. Such phenomena have not infrequently occurred in the history of religion, of the arts and of politics. For example, the relatively inert and seemingly outmoded doctrine of Marxism thus came after half a century to dominate the whole cultural and political apparatus of a large portion of the earth.

Within the total cultural heritage the ever-increasing growth of science and technology plays a special role. It far outstrips the ability of any mind to grasp as a whole, but every area of this immense territory is not only within the range of some group of specialists but also is recorded in the immortality of the printed word. The incessant resort to this fund of accumulative knowledge provides a basis of continuity that nothing can undermine. Science with its attendant technology, while a mainspring of change, superseding old habits and sometimes confounding old doctrines, is at the same time an all-pervasive system with persistent trends, establishing its own characteristic schema of relationships across the earth. The storehouse of research and scientific discovery has resources that are sometimes neglected or forgotten, to be rediscovered and utilized at a later time. One of many instances is the genetic law of Mendel which after a generation had passed became integrated, with important consequences both theoretical and practical, into the operative body of biological science.

Thus through the cultural heritage in the arts, the humanities and the sciences, we have continuity in depth, continuity sustained not only by the forces of the moving present but also by the resurgence of influences uprising from the deeps of the past.

The special feature of this continuity in depth is the power of *recall*. There is a parallel here between the continuity of personality and that of society. Sometimes through mere association, sometimes to sustain a present mood, sometimes in reverie or sentimental recollection, sometimes to compare new experiences with older ones or to facilitate or guide decision in the face of new problems—for one reason or another we summon up remembrance of things past. In like manner society, in its everyday business as well as on historical occasions, draws on its files and its archives, its stores of accumulated experience, the great cultural deposits of the ages. The recall may be dim or clear, accurate or blurred by sentiment or interest, judiciously selective or capricious, but one way or another it weaves its network of relationship between the changing present and the changeless past.

One way in which social man reaffirms his continuity with his past is through the orderly use of our third category, succession. Social life, especially in its more developed types, is knit in a web of organization. Without this organization there could be no established order, no developed economy, no advancement of science, nothing beyond the most primitive, insecure, chaotic and poverty-stricken life. Its institutions are the bulwark of every society. They do not pass away like mortal men. They have an indefinitely long and always renewable tenure. This perpetuity is generated by the principle of succession. It may be a natural linkage, as in the family or the tribe where kinship knits the generations; monarchical succession is another example. Or it may be a contrived linkage, as in the various forms of nomination, appointment and election. All kinds of devices have been tried to meet the major problem of political government —the combination of effective leadership and, with it, assurance against the arbitrary use of power—though none has proven more than partially successful.

Succession, then, is the way in which man's mortality is reconciled to the perpetuance of his institutions, while at the same time it is the way in which every younger generation seeks to keep these institutions from hardening into bureaucratic fixity.

Finally, just as man devises forms of succession, so he makes or organizes recurrences and for similar ends. The most obvious way is by resort to the calendar. George Washington was born on the twenty-second of February, 1732. Every twenty-second of February becomes for us an anniversary, the occasion for a national holiday and patriotic ovations. So we link the present moment to a moment long gone by. Again, we not infrequently magnify the element of recurrence in new situations in order to satisfy some emotional need. In other words, we turn new situations into the simulacra of old ones, converting partial resemblances into full-bodied recurrences. When something breaks into our habituations, disrupting our ways and our thoughts, we may endeavor to alleviate its impact by recalling a similar situation we lived through once before. "It is not worse than that," we think; "perhaps not so bad." "Endure my heart," cried the Homeric hero in his dire plight; "you have endured an even more doggish thing." From a variety of motivations, from sentiment, for reassurance, to make adjustment easier we discover that the new situation is but an old one in disguise.

Memory is too much the servant of need to be a reliable register of what has been. Memory provides another time dimension of consciousness, not as a mere record keeper or storehouse of information but as the great integrator of the total personality, sustaining its essential oneness over time. But in doing so it is implicated in the struggle of this personality to assert itself, to justify itself, to satisfy its wants, to fulfill its impulses. And so the record it keeps is not only subject to lapses and inadequacies but is also liable to the glosses and partialities of an over-friendly witness.

Consequently no man can, however good his faith,

write a faithful life history. One might add that no history whatever, whether of a nation or of a family, whether it covers a few years or some centuries, can give a really accurate account of what has been. All history suffers from the inadequate recall, the selective concern, the limited angle of vision and the faulty communication of the contemporary witnesses, and all later historians must not only struggle to interpret the records and draw their often quite variant inferences but must also do so under changed conditions and in another climate of opinion. As for an individual's own life history, the fact that emotions cannot be conjured up by the memory conspires with the bias of recollection and the forgetfulness of later years. Much of the truth that time has buried can never be resurrected.

VII

THE CHANGING FACE OF TIME

'Thus we may see,' quoth he, 'how the world
wags:
'Tis but an hour ago since it was nine;
And after one more hour 'twill be eleven.'
—WILLIAM SHAKESPEARE, *As You Like It*

As we grow older the ceaseless mergence of the present in the future becomes more importunate, and the lapse of the present into the past more weighted with finality. It would seem that the longer the memory span, the shorter becomes each passing day. As the past lengthens for us, the memories of it crowd the subconscious mind and lie ever near to the surface. The future becomes less visionary, more calculable but less secure. The blending of memories with anticipations, the emotions with which we recall the past and approach the future, are subject to continuous change.

A primary condition in the changing feel of life is the changing face of time. In this chapter we shall endeavor to sketch the main attitudinal differences attending the stages of our time journey.

In childhood the moments occupy us almost wholly, with scarcely any forethought and scarcely a backward glance. Our emotions are fleeting, and we pass from tears to laughter without transition. Our wants are immediate and urgent. Our expectations and dreads are rooted in

33

the primacy of the moment. Experience is episodic. The immediate scene is the whole world, an unpatterned whirr of sensuous and visceral perceptions. The child is a mimic. And its early learning comes through imitating the ways, the gestures and the sounds of the elders. Its relationships are idiocentric responses of approbation or disapprobation to what is done or not done to satisfy the call of its bodily needs.

Gradually the child comes to distinguish its own self-hood and in degree to recognize the selfhood of others. Its horizons expand; the near space becomes a continuity, and time becomes a stretch from the now to the then. The future begins to have a significance not limited by the expectations based on the needs of the present hour. The recognition of an ampler future is stimulated by the injunctions of parents and others. "If you want to become a big strong boy, you'd better take your medicine." "If you don't learn your lessons, you'll be sorry someday." "What are you going to be when you grow up?" And so forth. The present has begun to demand the future.

Another way the significance of time is impressed on the young child is through the principle of seniority. Between him and his parents the gap of time is so incalculably great as to be beyond conception, but his brother, say, or the boy next door is in a higher grade at school because he is two years older. The senior boy is bigger and stronger, can do more things; the younger boy looks up to him. That's what growing up means. Seniority plays a major role in the associations of children. In fact it has a value very much like that which it has in primitive kin-bound societies or in highly bureaucratized organizations not unknown to ourselves.

We remark in passing that while childhood is a period of learning and being trained for the activities of the future, it is also a highly important part of our time for living. No more than for any other period should the claims of the future abrogate the claims of the present. Childhood has its own proper life, its own joys, its own griefs, its own world of experience. In the eyes of grownups its blisses may be pigmy blisses, but to the child they have a fresh and wonderful radiance. The discipline and the training children need should not pre-empt the satisfactions that belong to childhood and to childhood alone.

In adolescence the future takes on a new significance. For a number of reasons the youth is now compelled to look ahead. The young man—and now, with much greater frequency than before, the young woman—enter the work-a-day world or else begin the specific preparation for a profession or other career. The present takes on a definite responsibility for the future. The claim of the future receives another great stimulus, since the normal youth is preoccupied with sex relations and sooner or later recognizes their implication for the future. Nevertheless there is a strong urge in youth at this stage to give free play to its new impulses, to drink the wine of life in the present. This situation creates the major dilemma we expose in a succeeding chapter.

Adolescence is a time of disturbance. New opportunities are crossed by new problems. Habits formed in childhood and earlier youth no longer fit the new conditions. There are prospects of a fuller life, but there are also intimations of narrowing horizons. Marriage will mean settling down and earning more money. With anticipated new satisfactions there are also suggestions of the shades of the prison house.

For the young woman the stage inaugurated by puberty brings still more drastic changes. The outlook on the *near* future becomes generally all-engrossing. There is a ferment of new emotions and new anticipations. The emotions center about the business of being in love, and the central quest is for the reciprocity that would make the love relationship the gateway to the fulfillments that come through marriage. Her attitude toward the near future is more concentrated and less complicated by conflicting considerations than that of the young man. Perhaps particularly in middle-class circles she regards the years immediately ahead as crucial for a whole lifetime. Differences of economic and social status modify this attitude, but the reactions indicated are as nearly general as any characterization that can be made concerning the ways of human beings.

The combination of biological and social factors has demarcated the life stages of women much more sharply than those of men. Puberty comes with its early bloom heralding a greatly changed relationship to the world of men. Marriage and childbearing thrust on the woman an entirely new type of responsibility and function. The change of life has again its determinate time. In earlier times the period of bloom was short and that of childbearing long, and when youth ended, the woman quickly aged. In our modern civilization the calendar of the years has still its special significance for women, but the severity of the transitions has been progressively reduced by a variety of factors—the greater freedom accorded to women; the prolongation of youthfulness through dietetic and hygienic advances; the business-world employment of married women; the limitation of child-bearing and other developments.

Once adulthood becomes fully established with the fixation of work habits and mode-of-life routines, time's changes become less decisive over a relatively long period. Time becomes a continuum with a slow gradient toward aging, roughened by events and an occasional crisis. Generally it is held to be the time of maturity, though what maturity implies may not be clear. Middle-aged people usually—there are of course exceptions due to illness, inertia or adverse conditions—think of themselves as still young. The adolescent regards the man of thirty as already old, and the old man regards the middle-aged as youngsters.

But during the continuum of middle age some signs of the increasing years obtrude themselves. Gray hairs and deeper wrinkles and heavier tread and less agile motions herald the nearness of old age. Birthdays arrive at a more unseemly rate. Acquaintances betray the evidences of aging we may be less ready to admit in ourselves. Now and again the passing of a friend or a relative affirms the sufferance on which we hold our tenure of life. Those whom we regarded as striplings are occupying prominent places in the world of affairs. We begin to be treated as elders.

It is in this period, however, that the significant disparity between the aging of the body and the aging of the mind gives us new comfort. The timing of intellectual maturity is highly variant, both with respect to the age at which it is attained and with respect to its duration. In many instances the maturity of the mind comes later than the full development of physical capacities, and quite often it endures even to an advanced age. Some of the greatest achievements in the sciences and in such arts as poetry, the novel, sculpture and architecture have been the work of men approaching or even exceeding three-score and ten. Leaders in politics and in the world of affairs are frequently elderly men, though no doubt other considerations than ability have here to be taken into account.

The fact that intellectual capacity need not and often does not diminish with the decline of physical capacity, and indeed may even increase well after the zenith of physical prowess is passed, suggests some far-reaching considerations concerning the nature of human evolution. In the present context one passing comment may be relevant. The fact before us discomfits a favorite analogy used to illustrate the life process. It is thought of as having the form of an arc, a half circle, that ascends gradually, reaches its high point and then gradually descends. Men love to find simple rhythms or symmetries in the ordering of things. And so man's life is conceived of as passing from nothingness to fullness and back to nothingness, the second half of the arc repeating the first in reverse. There is of course some resemblance here, but the life course submits itself to no such easy patterning, as is shown by the signal evidence of older people in the arts and sciences as well as in the conduct of affairs.

Old age itself—like every other stage of life's journey—proves different from our prior conception of it. If a measure of health remains, it does not rob us of the joys of living, though it adds some inconveniences and curtails some former pleasures. The speed of reactions to signals is slowed, and there is usually some deterioration of vision and of hearing and some impairment of memory. But there are ways of making a reasonably effective adjustment to these conditions which still permit the old, where opportunity is given, to share the satisfactions of active life.

The old are likely to become more resigned to things as they are or at least as they have learned to think they are. They cease to be surprised at the hastening pace of the calendar. Every added year is a bonus. All they can hope for is a few more years, and they come to regard the tale of years as itself honorific. Of all life's periods old age is the least prospective. Like children, the old may live almost wholly by the hour and the day, but their dreams are of the past and not of the future. Curiosity has nothing more to feed on, and however the world changes, there is nothing new under the sun. For better or worse the course has been run. The ambitions that spurred us and remain unattained are no longer an itch. And where there are fewer expectations, there are also fewer fears.

In this sketch of the attitudes to time that characterize the various "ages" of man we have taken no account of the exceptions and variations that differences of health, disposition, lot in life, fortune and faith evoke. Nor have we suggested the complexities of mood and feeling that attend the typical reactions, we have indicated. In some later chapters we shall look at certain expedients to which people resort in the endeavor to accommodate themselves to the inexorable processes of their journeying through time.

VIII

THE RELATIVITY OF CONSCIOUS TIME

> *Time travels in divers paces with divers persons. I'll tell you who Time ambles withal, who Time trots withal, who Time gallops withal, and who Time stands still withal.*
>
> —WILLIAM SHAKESPEARE, *As You Like it*

H<small>OW LONG</small> is a day, an hour, a year? Too short for what? Too long for what? Sometimes we wish the hour would end. Often we wish the day were longer. Now the time drags. Now it's over all too soon for our enjoyment of it, too soon for the work we want to do.

Clock time, the register of the minutes as they add up to days and years and centuries, is the common measure of age for all things, animate or inanimate. But the measure of age is not the measure of process, since that varies endlessly. And the significance of time is precisely its relation to change. Hence clock time is an inadequate index for many of our purposes. We must, for example, draw a distinction between biological age and chronological age. Two human beings who are equally old by the calendar may be quite unequally old in the organism's register of age. Again, what is a short spell of time for one creature may be very long for another. A day is a lifetime for the ephemerid but a mere breathing space for the elephant. Change is the process from one state to another. For the living it is the process that begins with birth and ends in death. They all

40

pass through a similar series of stages of greatly varying length according to their kind and their circumstance. Analogously, we speak of the life of an inanimate object as being relatively long or relatively short, measured by a standard appropriate to its kind. Thus the meson, a particle that emerges from high-energy collisions in the accelerator of the physicist, lives less than a millionth of a second, but atomic scientists speak of this life as relatively long "compared to the millionth of a billionth of a billionth of a second it takes for products of their decay to move apart." [1] There could hardly be a more striking example of one aspect of the relativity of time.

Conscious time, time as reckoned by the conscious being, has another kind of relativity. In two equal spaces of clock time the quantity and quality of living may be very different, and the hours pass more quickly or more slowly accordingly. In general, they pass more quickly when we are engrossed or excited or when the emotional tone is smoothly pleasant or when we indulge in quiet reverie. They pass more slowly when we are bored or when waiting impatiently for some anticipated event or when we feel anxiety or when we are in pain or in anguish. But there are many variations and complexities in this mental estimate of time. The intensity of our engrossment and the span of our attention make a considerable difference. It is also complicated by the physiological changes that accompany or stimulate our mental attitudes, by the state of our nervous system, by the way the heart beats, by the metabolism rate and so forth.

In a wider sense the manner of life we are accustomed to lead affects the reckoning. If we are attuned to a leisurely mode of life or to one of a simple steady-going kind, such as the life of the shepherd or of a village craftsman,

[1] Robert Oppenheimer, "The Mystery of Matter," *Adventures of the Mind,* ed. Thruesen and Kobler (New York: Alfred A. Knopf, Inc., 1960).

we are less concerned with the passage of the hours than if we were engaged in the competitive life of the city. If we live in the cloister, the tinkling of the bell may remind us not so much of time as of a duty or devotion. We speak of the tempo of living, and the word tempo is accurate— it is the pace at which our time goes, as reckoned by the mental chronometer.

A curious phenomenon has been observed in studies of prolonged unemployment. In the early stages men out of work are likely to be somewhat restive or expectant and frequently try to occupy themselves in some kind of activity. But where unemployment becomes habitual and no alternative jobs open up, the attitude undergoes a change. In a study made of a locality in Austria in which all the workers were rendered idle for a considerable length of time because of the closing down of the single factory in the place, it was found that the men became increasingly tardy in returning home for such scant meals as their women were enabled to provide, much to the vexation of the latter.

A biochemist friend of mine made an interesting discovery. Once when his wife ran a temperature of 104, he hurried to the drugstore for some medicine, returning in around ten minutes. She declared he had been away at least half an hour and persisted in saying so in spite of his denials. Suddenly an idea struck him: perhaps in her fevered state she had a different time register than normally. Her fevered brain was in more rapid motion than usual. Its excessive activity made ten minutes, as commonly experienced, into thirty or more. Testing this hypothesis in various ways with hospital patients having high temperatures, he was able to find adequate confirmation of it. Our normal time reckoning is accommodated to the more usual state of the brain and the nerve centers. Ten minutes of ordinary conscious time may well count up to thrice that number when fever is high.

Other evidences for the relativity of conscious time are derived from the phenomena of dreams, reveries, and hallucinatory states. In dreams brain impulses follow a different pattern from that of the waking world, and the electric currents that course through the brain are greatly modified. In the dream world there is only a present time; past incidents reappear as happening in the now; past events are relived with the peculiar foreshortenings and distortions of dream experience. What happened over years seems to be occurring anew in the sequence of brief dream moments.

The magical pace of happenings in the dream world is used in support of the theory that the dream itself, though it may cover quite a range of scenes and emotions, occurs actually in the brief period of transition from sleeping to waking. This position, however, is not well founded. There are reasons to believe that the dream may occupy a considerable spell of time and also that even in deep sleep dream processes are present, though the memory retains no record of them. One fairly obvious indication is that some dreamers can be heard to speak in their dreams, to speak at the rate of their ordinary speech.

In other respects dreams play fast and loose with the realities of the waking life. The conditions of actual travel through space, just as of travel through time, no longer hold. We can be in one place this moment and hundreds of miles away the next, just as we can relive a situation of far-back days and immediately thereafter return to some episodes of yesterday—or the two situations may even merge into one. In dreams we see ourselves doing feats impossible for us in actuality, and on the other hand we sometimes find ourselves unaccountably unable to perform the simplest action, such as running away from an impending peril. The actions and inactions of our dreams are detached from the motor responses of waking life.

In hypnotic and hallucinatory states, as in the special

dream worlds induced by various narcotics, time has different reckonings than that of the daily round. Sometimes it is as though time did not exist, as though our travel through it were suspended and the moment lived on. In the account given of one experience with a hallucinogenic mushroom that is found in a remote area of Mexico and is the basis of a sacred ritual for the initiates, the narrator writes of the remarkable visions produced by the drug, of the sense of floating free in air and of a great liberation from the limits of everyday experience. He and his companion spent "two timeless nights in almost complete darkness." While the mushrooms tend to sharpen the memory, "they utterly destroy the sense of time. On the night that we have described we lived through eons. When it seemed to us that a sequence of visions had lasted for years, our watches would tell us that only seconds had passed." [1]

The mental states we have just referred to are different from that of the dream proper. The subjects may still be aware—but with a difference—of their surroundings. In some directions their senses may be sharpened, although their perception of clock time is stilled. They are for a time living, as it were, in a new unrealized world of their own, attuned to the change in their senses and their emotions. It is one that so wholly commands them that they are oblivious of the hours ticked off on the clock.

Without benefit of drugs we may reach the borders of these more visionary states, sometimes under the influence of overpowering emotions but sometimes along the quiet path of reverie. We speak of being "lost in thought" when we are absorbed in a kind of dreamy reflection, forgetful of our surroundings. Reverie is the effortless review, in a mood of withdrawal from sense perceptions, of events or situations or problems that emerge in the subconscious.

---

[1] R. Gordon Wasson, "Seeking the Magic Mushroom," *Life*, May 13, 1957, p. 100.

It is a mood in which the mind moves freely and is led by association from one theme to another, an inconsequent mood that ends far from the thought with which it began. It is the dream of the subconscious self when it reaches the threshold of wakefulness. But, like the deep dream and the hypnotic sleep, it measures time by a different standard than we do in our waking life.

A modern writer has remarked that "the unconscious has its own clock." He was not thinking of the dream world but of the way in which so often a new discovery, a new idea, a new faith does not emerge into any recognition of its significance until years or generations after it was first announced. Mendel's law was ignored for the best part of a generation; the significance of Darwinism took many years to be realized. Christianity waited for centuries before it caught the imagination of more than a small group. There are endless illustrations. The portent of the atomic bomb, the case to which our author (Arthur Koestler) particularly refers, was for the most part regarded at first as merely a more murderous weapon added to the already dreadful arsenal of war. Now we are beginning to understand that it marks the parting of the ways, the most tremendous choice between a new epoch in which either the eternal poverty of the greater portion of mankind will be abolished or one in which the earth itself will suffer total desolation. Our author presents a different aspect of this awakening recognition. "Hitherto man had to live with the idea of his death as an individual; from now onward mankind will have to live with the idea of its death as a species." In his view the period of unconscious "incubation" is coming to an end.

Leaving aside this larger speculation of an unconscious time system in which ideas and philosophies ripen in the minds of groups or whole societies, we have ample evidence that the inner measurement of time is relative and varies according to age, condition and mode of life. By inner measurement we mean the relative sense of duration in the conscious being, so that the same span of clock time will feel longer or shorter as these factors differ. Moreover, there are conditions and moods in which the sense of the passing of time is wholly absent.

Nor can we say that any one of the variant measurements of conscious time is more real, more true than another. We are prone to believe that the clock measures real time, whereas it directly measures only the equal stages in a process of uniform motion. But the conscious assessment of the lapse of time will be longer or shorter according to our condition. It is then *really* longer or shorter for us.

Our dream experience is, while we dream, entirely real, the only real. When we waken from a threatening dream, we realize with a sense of relief that it was only a dream. We were deluded into regarding as reality the precipice we were about to fall over or the wild beast we were being pursued by or whatever other evil was upon us. Such experiences have supported a notion that claims to have more philosophical grounds, the notion that it is never reality we experience but only the impressions and the visions and the thoughts evoked in our consciousness by a reality to which we can never probe. Our waking life is but a dream on a "higher" level. The myths of our everyday world are more enduring, more directly evoked by sense impressions, more rationalized than the echo impressions of our sleep. "We are such stuff as dreams are made on," and like the dreams from which we awaken to find they were the mere play of our uneasy minds, so could we awaken from the dream of life, we would find that it too was as insubstantial as a cloud castle. It would then follow that, as a well-known poem puts it,

> Each age is a dream that is dying,
> Or one that is coming to birth.

Time is the greatest of all human mysteries, and whichever way we think about it, we end in an impasse, faced by some great intriguing question to which no answer is forthcoming, since we find no road between the question and its exploration.

IX

A MAJOR DILEMMA

> *One Moment in Annihilation's Waste*
> *One Moment, of the Well of Life to taste—*
> *The Stars are setting, and the Caravan*
> *Starts for the Dawn of Nothing—Oh, make*
>   *haste.*   —OMAR KHAYYÁM, *Rubáiyát*

AMONG the simplest facts about life are three facts concerning time. These facts are eternally valid and admit no possible exceptions. Taken together they pose a multitude of problems, and in particular they confront civilized man with a major dilemma. We say civilized man, since the alternatives in question have little application where the vast majority live at subsistence level.

One of these three facts is the irreversibility of time or rather of our passage through time. We can never return over the road we have traveled to the present. What has once been done, what has once happened can never be recalled. The spoken word cannot be unspoken or the accomplished act rescinded. Time does not erase history; it merely buries it.

A second fact is that we cannot halt for one moment our journeying through time. If we journey wisely, we may journey longer, but there are no roadside retreats. Watch the second hand travel through one minute—that unresting pace continues without end. We are always a day older by the calendar than we were yesterday. Conscious time, as we have insisted, has a different reckoning from that of the clock, but the experience it reckons moves unceasingly on.

The third fact gives poignancy to the other two. Our onward march through time is not to a goal, not to a destination, but to a finality. Young or old, we are equally under sentence of death. Whether we regard death as annihilation or believe in a life beyond, we go the same road thither. And every tick of the clock brings us nearer to that hour.

Our sense of values is greatly concerned and inextricably interwoven with this trinity of facts. The responses we make to them vary with our dispositions, our circumstances and our indoctrinations, but the worthwhileness of all our objectives, however they may vary, must sooner or later be reckoned in the perspective these facts provide. Some face them straightly, anchored in their convictions. Others give them only an occasional uneasy glance, so as not to disturb overmuch the course they pursue. Others propitiate the inevitable by resort to certain rituals and formulas that mitigate the need for further concern.

All in all, these facts are too insistent not to bite deeply into the emotions of men. The sense of life's brevity gives edge and urgency to some of our desires and deflates the worthwhileness of others, but again how it affects us is extremely variant.

The all-engrossing activity of the vast majority of living things is focused on the sustaining of life—seeking food, reproducing its kind, rearing its offspring, escaping the enemies that would devour it since these, too, must live. Life and death are as inseparable as light and darkness, but of that relationship only human beings have any inkling. The knowledge of it brings tragedy into life and evokes spiritual yearnings that transcend the business of living. Along with tragedy come the greater virtues and the greater vices. With it are associated heroism and high purpose and the quest for the divine, and with it, too, come craven fears and the dissolution of incentive. The trinity of time-facts turn life into an ever changing drama, with color and suspense, with catastrophe and with triumph, with pity and terror and self-abnegating love.

Among the other features of this many-centered drama is that it frequently poses for each actor in it a certain dilemma, at times a major dilemma, especially for the younger members of the ever renewed cast. At every turn the broad alternatives are the same. Shall we take the cash and let the credit go? Shall we choose the immediate boon or work instead for the remoter but greater reward? The immediate boon may be each passing gratification that diverts us from the pursuit of more enduring satisfactions. Or the choice may be presented as one between an assured return and one that might be considerably larger but involves delay, abstinence and risk. Or it may be starkly set as one between easy indulgence and arduous duty, the latter being presumptively the condition of a more worthy life. Or it may be the option of a selfish advantage at the cost of another's pain or loss, implying, no doubt, the disregard of the adverse effect on one's character and reputation.

While there are many kinds of recurrent situations in which the dilemma appears, the crucial cases are those where the choice is once and for all. One example is the situation in which a young person has to decide whether to undergo a protracted period of training for, say, a scientific or professional career, enduring present poverty and the discipline of preparation, or to enter an immediately available employment. How one discounts future goods— to use the term of the economist—varies endlessly according to disposition and to the urgency of present need.

The characteristic literature directed to this dilemma divides sharply into two camps. On the one hand there is the literature, sometimes gay and carefree, but often tinged with melancholy, that extols the sweet and evanescent pleasures of youth and bids us enjoy them while yet there

is time. "Youth's a stuff will not endure." One thing you
cannot save is time; therefore make the most of it. To postpone the pleasures of today is to lose them forever. The
pleasures they speak of are the sensuous pleasures, summed
up in the expression, "wine, women and song." Sometimes
the exhortation is in metaphorical language:

"Come down, oh maid, from yonder mountain height.
What pleasure lives in cold? The shepherd sang."

A typical example is the well-known lines of Herrick:

"Gather ye rosebuds while ye may
Old Time is still a-flying,
And this same flower that smiles today
To-morrow may be dying."

In the more melancholy form there is combined lament for
the brevity of our joys and exhortation to discount the
future so that we may fully possess them today.

From similar premises the opposing camp reaches flatly
opposite conclusions. Yes, the time is short and youth
soon passes, but all the more important is it that youth
should be the time of preparation for a life directed to
serious ends. It is the time when habits are formed and
character is molded. The most grievous waste is the waste
of this precious time when it is frittered away in pleasure
or dissipated in indulgence.

The more religiously minded tend to regard the pursuit
of pleasures as not only a defection from the demands of a
virtuous life but also as a violation of God's law. The most
formidable pronouncement along this line is the passage
in *Ecclesiastes:*

"Rejoice, O young man, in thy youth; and let thy heart
cheer thee in the days of thy youth, and walk in the ways

of thine heart, and in the sight of thine eyes; but know thou, that for all these things God will bring thee into judgment."

In less grim tones than those of the preacher youth is told that pleasures are deceiving as well as short-lived. "You seize the flower, its bloom is shed." Abiding satisfactions are to be found only through the discipline that builds life into a unity of purpose.

Obviously these opposite pronouncements, with their many variations, are animated by different assumptions concerning the nature and destiny of man. Some of the attitudes toward time that are thus engendered will be reviewed in later chapters. No matter what our assumptions, however, the dilemma still intrudes. The youth who is minded to follow the admonitions of the preacher still meets not infrequent situations where he must decide between an immediate return and the uncertain prospect of something more attractive. The follower of the "wine, women and song" prescription must still weigh the consequences of yielding to the temptation of the hour, since the consequences may grossly interfere with the prospect of the pleasures yet to come. And the great majority of human beings, who are not fully committed to any such exclusive principles, are constantly faced with the decision between the nearer tempting advantage and the farther goal.

Our attitudes to every aspect of our journey through time are obviously dependent on our scheme of values in the push and pull of our desires, but one consideration underlying our decisions is always in the background—the brevity of time. This thought moves the devout to redeem the time while yet the opportunity is theirs as well as to exhort other men that "now is the time for salvation." It spurs the pleasure lover to make the most of the hours while yet enjoyment is within his grasp. It brings a gnawing sense of impotence to those who see life slipping by without the realization of their ambitions. It gives urgency to the creative minds who fear they may not live to complete the work they yearn to accomplish. So Keats, who died at twenty-six, exclaimed:

> "O for ten years, that I may overwhelm
> Myself in poesy; so I may do the deed
> That my own soul has to itself decreed."

It makes the dictator tremble lest in his failing years the sceptre may be snatched from his grasp by some younger rival. And the aging hero of many accomplishments still feels the urge to add one more.

> "Death closes all: but something ere the end.
> Some work of noble note, may yet be done."

PART THREE

Reactions to the Calendar

X

THE OBSESSION OF THE PASSING PRESENT

> *Whatever withdraws us from the power of the senses; whatever makes the past, the distant, or the future predominate over the present advances us in the dignity of thinking beings.*
> —SAMUEL JOHNSON, *Inch Kenneth*

IN THE pronouncement cited above, the oracular dictionary-maker takes in characteristic fashion his stand in favor of one of the various ways in which men react to the passing of the years. We have noted how at different stages of the life course the past, the present and the future are seen through different eyes. Aside from such broad distinctions—the very young absorbed in the present, the adolescent looking ahead, old age returning to the world of memories and so forth—there are various types of action responses evoked by the hastening years. Some people are particularly concerned over the brevity of the time immediately before them in which to seize fleeting pleasures or meet some impending needs or demands. Oth-

55

ers are more or less content to find at each stage of life its own appropriate satisfactions and responsibilities or at the least are resigned to accept, as in the natural order of things, the presumptive time limits of life's successive activities and enjoyments. Others again follow a diagonal between these two opposing modes, not exhibiting the sense of pressure the first entails nor resting in the comparative acquiescence of the second, but finding one way or another of mitigating a never wholly absent concern over the transience of life.

One or other of these three modes is in the ascendant for human beings over a considerable portion of their lives, with occasional deflections into one of the other two. As we shall presently see, persons of extremely different disposition in other respects will nevertheless, in their respective ways, conform to the same mode. Each of the three may be exhibited to any degree, from the mildest tendency in its direction to a pathological extreme. In the discussions to follow we shall dwell particularly on the more pronounced manifestations.

Our first mode, the urgency to exploit the near opportunities that may soon enough cease to be ours, offers ample illustrations of the diversity of objectives that alternatively, in accord with differences of disposition, make imperative claims on the present. We have already dwelt on one form of this mode, the urgency summed up in the ancient expression: "Let us eat and drink; for tomorrow we shall die." It is most frequently, though by no means only, the youthful who are exhorted to snatch those pleasures of which the years will rob them.

The attitude here indicated is to be distinguished from one that merely laments the quick transience of the beauty and the strength of youth. What is common to the two is the conviction that youth, the season of bloom, is beyond compare the best, and that no later rewards can any way compensate for the loss of it. To some it is the time of high

aspirations, brave visions and generous impulses. Words-
worth, for example, in the famous ode on *Intimations of
Immortality,* represents youth as still possessing the "vision
splendid" that later fades into the "light of common day."
Some are content to hymn the praise of youth as the spring-
time of life when all the world is fresh and fair. With this
attitude goes the sentiment that those who die young escape
the disillusionments and sorrows of later years. They are
those "whom the gods love." The soldiers who may fall in
warfare are "the lads who will die in their glory and never
grow old."

In contrast to these more brooding attitudes there is the
urge to exploit to the full, before it is too late, the opportunities of the present. In one form it is expressed in the
words, "Youth's the season made for joys." The exclusive
stress it lays on these particular joys easily becomes an
obsession discounting the other potentialities of youth and
thus ignoring the satisfactions of the present and, still more,
those of the future that attend the development of the potentialities. With its greedy grasp of the immediate boon,
it tends to identify the shallow gratification of quickly won
sensations with the full enjoyment of life, rejecting the
deeper-ranging reward attainable through enlistment in
causes that transcend any concern for immediate pleasure.

The present-tense urgency, reaching up to the level of
an obsession, has, however, some extremely different expressions. The urgency may be motivated by the brevity of
the time within which one can make some essential preparation for the future. For everyone some conjunctures arise
that call for the primacy of present action to meet some
impending demand. And there come stages in the life history of individuals or of groups when present provision to
ensure some long-term objective is imperative. Obviously
we would not deem obsessive any reasonable preoccupation so directed. There is, say, the young woman whose
overriding concern is to find and win a desirable mate,

and there is the young man who "scorns delights and lives laborious days" to win a scholarship that will open for him the road to a coveted career.

The urgency of the present need becomes an extreme form of obsession in the case of the miser—the type of miser who, having learned under the stresses of early poverty not to squander the pennies, has hardened into blind avarice when there is no further call for such narrow saving and continues to clutch every reachable dollar for no end whatever except accumulation, walled within the comfortless and friendless prison of his empty habit. Thus his whole existence becomes futile preparation against the necessities of an imaginary future. The end has been lost in the means.

Some degree of the same type of obsession may be attributed to those who unduly postpone the time when they can devote themselves to what they regard as worthwhile ends or the time when they propose to get more enjoyment out of living. Having been obligated earlier to acquire the means for such ends, they become so engrossed in the competitive struggle that the promised release is always being postponed until it fades altogether from the prospect. The struggle that was once exacting now has grown absorbing. At length it becomes their life. The means has changed into the end for which it is sought, means to more means forever.

The cases we have been considering are illustrations of a very common experience, in which the once prospective future, the goal of early days, becomes dimmed or altogether forgotten. Sometimes it is due to the sheer necessities of livelihood. Often it is because the habits engendered in the pursuit of the means conspire with ambitions fostered by the pursuit, the ambitions of status, of position and of power, so that these newer ambitions block out the older aspirations. In the area of the fine arts this tendency may take on a more subtle character, undermining the quality of work and at length reducing imagination to technical skill in order that the popularity of the artist may be upheld and his precarious future made more secure. For this end he will give the public what it seems to want instead of what he might have it in him to give. For this end he may stick to the pattern of his first success instead of giving his power of invention free play. Scientists and scholars generally are not always immune to a similar temptation. More obvious, perhaps, is the case of the careerist in politics who sheds his principles and becomes the spokesman for the crowd or for the interests that can best protect his future. Such are some of the many ways in which the drive for future security or material advantage diverts the goals to which men devote themselves.

Finally, let us consider a situation in which high goals themselves, projected toward some future fulfilment, may become so peremptory that they require the abandonment of the present pleasures of living, not for a period only but for the whole span of the lifetime—and sometimes such goals may call for not merely the sacrifice of pleasures but even the self-infliction of discomforts and pains. The future that makes these demands is reached through the gate of death, but since this future is deemed to be eternal and blessed, the abstinences and negations it requires are not to be reckoned against the reward. Various religions induce such attitudes in their most dedicated followers. The call may be for a vow of poverty, for the repudiation of earthbound pleasures, for the abstention from all sexual relationships, for total withdrawal from the world. The histories of Hinduism, Judaism, Christianity and some other creeds offer endless examples of the different modes and degrees in which the call is made and accepted.

XI

THE READINESS FOR CHANGE

To live is to change, and to be perfect is to have changed often.

—CARDINAL NEWMAN, *Discourses on Religion*

AMONG the variant responses to the inexorable call of the years, we consider here those that take the transitions of life with some measure of acceptance. At one end of the range there are those adventurous spirits—a small enough group—who, like Ulysses, might be said to "take with a frolic welcome the thunder and the sunshine." There are others who are temperamentally ready to make the best of things, being more disposed to adapt themselves to new conditions than to mourn for the old ones. There are some who, Micawber-like, are always expecting that something will turn up, some little bit of luck, some windfall. And there are the more passive-minded who take what comes in a spirit of acquiescence or resignation.

We are concerned here with attitudes characteristic of people not on favorable occasions only but throughout the greater portion of their lives. Everyone welcomes change when it is in accord with his desires, but it requires a particular type of disposition to accommodate itself to change no matter what it brings.

There is, first, the buoyant attitude that looks forward with expectancy and rides over vicissitudes without serious disturbance. While this attitude is more commonly displayed through the earlier stages of life and may lose its vigor before the troubles of later years, there are some who display it persistently to the end. As in youth they move gladly toward manhood, as in full manhood they anticipate new opportunities and pursue new attainments, so in their later years the thought of retirement and new leisure has no attraction for them, but instead they find some way of carrying on and have their eyes still fixed on further horizons.

No doubt we can all instance persons of this type. As a somewhat remarkable example we take Robert Browning, who not only exhorted us to welcome each rebuff "that turns earth's smoothness rough," but went so far as to say, referring to old age and death,

> The best is yet to be
> The last of life for which the first was made,

and then called death the joyous opening of the gate to reunion with his beloved. We may find a touch of romantic bravado in Browning's attitude, but undoubtedly the whole tenor of his work is the expression under all conditions of a stalwart, forward-looking spirit.

A different mode of expectancy that also looks beyond the end of life is entertained by those religious-minded people who accept the tenets of their faith with sufficient conviction to believe that "the better life is there," that the tribulations they face are to be cheerfully endured as the trials of this preparatory existence, since when these are over the joys of paradise lie ahead. This other mode, however, is likely to be less robust or more quiescent than the former, since the prospect is one that cannot be envisaged and for the ordinary mortal is often enough clouded by dim questionings, by uneasy thoughts concerning so tremendous a transition and by the obstinate clinging of humans to the familiar world of flesh and blood as well as by occasional fears concerning the possibility of a *dies irae* (day of wrath). Oriental religions offer men no such transcendental alternatives of glory and terror, but instead for the most part the prospect either of eternal peace, the self-oblivion of nirvana's nothingness, or else of transmigration into some other form of earthly life, animal or human, in accord with the qualities displayed and developed in this previous existence.

Unlike those who expect the morrow to come bearing gifts, there are many—no doubt many more—who take the day for what it is and are prepared to take the morrow for what it may bring. They entertain neither the expectations of our former category nor the trepidations of those who have come to regard time as the great enemy. No doubt the multitudes who still live under peasant conditions, whose days are filled with endless, exacting toil simply to sustain life, are inured to accept whatever comes in a kind of fatalistic submission. Among ourselves there are those who display a similar attitude, who take as inevitable the vicissitudes of fortune and of time, who believe in luck—good luck and bad—and who have acquired a certain equanimity that makes them tolerably ready for change.

On another level of experience we find a more energetic type of preparedness. They are folk who have a fund of resiliency and are minded to make the best of things. When good times pass, when some pleasant relationship or enjoyable activity ends, when, say, their days as athletes or as elected officeholders are over, they are alert to find some new engrossment. In some such spirit the *bon vivant* poet Horace wrote an ode to tell the world that his time for love-making was through and that, like a returning warrior, he had now hung his armor on the wall. A person of this disposition easily consoles himself with other interests, finds ways of living more in keeping with new conditions and presently comes to think his later lot has advantages over the earlier one. The athlete, for example, turns into the coach or the sportswriter or the tavern-keeper perhaps. The ex-officeholder will have prepared himself for the practice of law, or he may attach himself to some corporation that can use his political experience. Such persons as we have in mind will readily change from time to time their mode of life and their occupational habits to meet whatever opportunities or needs present themselves. With relative ease they adapt themselves to the changing climate of their journeying through time.

The readiness for change of the kind of people we have been considering depends on mental resiliency—sometimes, we must add, also on moral flexibility. There is no deep commitment to earlier ways or earlier experiences. In this respect they stand at the opposite pole from another category, people who conform to a predetermined pattern that prescribes the appropriate activities for every season and for every stage of life. These are as inflexible in their way as our former category was flexible. With some the predestinate order is attributed simply to the nature of things, as understood by them; with others it is divine ordainment.

The latter viewpoint has its classic expression in the book of Ecclesiastes:

> To every thing there is a season, and a time to every purpose under the heaven: A time to be born, and a time to die; a time to plant, and a time to pluck up that which is planted; . . . a time to keep silence and a time to speak.

When it is nature that is credited with prescribing the allotted stages of life, men bow to a presumptive necessity—though the presumption itself may sometimes be the ground of the necessity. One cannot sin against a law of nature, and to make grievance of necessity is idle. One does not rebel against winter; it is the same law that brought the summer.

When on the other hand it is the divine order that legislates the season due, it becomes more a question of what is right and proper than of what is inevitable. We obey the higher code. There is a season for love and a season to refrain from loving, a season for feasting and a season for fasting. There is a time to put away childish things, a time for the sage contemplativeness of old age. In the rather puritanic environment in which the writer was brought up he has heard the gossiping group comment on the tendency of a lady in her forties to dress up and do her hair in the latest style: "The foolish creature! She should be thinking of her latter end." In somewhat this spirit the older peasant women of the region regularly wore dark shawls, often with white mutches over their heads. The dress symbolized the stage of life and the behavior proper to it.

The prescribed pattern made scant allowance for diversities of disposition or of vitality. The rigor of the pattern itself, however, was greater for women than for men, and divergences from it by the former met with more serious social opprobrium. There is of course nothing unusual in this sex distinction, which in degree holds practically everywhere. The characteristic feature is the determinateness of the time-patterning, such as in effect to preclude the continuation of certain activities beyond the age deemed proper for them. The period assigned to youth is short enough and the twilight of old age descends quickly. No doubt such prescriptions are calculated to induce a state of body as well as of mind congenial to them. We may suspect that a psychosomatic consequence in some instances is premature aging. And it may well be that our modern regulations concerning the age of compulsory retirement for industrial workers and various professional categories may work in the same direction.

XII

THE INDIFFERENT INTERVAL
AND OTHER PROTECTIONS

> *Time has no divisions to mark its passage, there*
> *is never a thunder-storm or blare of trumpets*
> *to announce the beginning of a new month or*
> *year. Even when a new century begins it is only*
> *we mortals who ring bells and fire off pistols.*
> —THOMAS MANN, *The Magic Mountain*

ANIMALS other than man appear oblivious of the fact that they grow older, and even the most intelligent of them may be unaware of their mortality. The provisions they make for the future and the continuance of their race are mostly not provisional but instinctive, the working of inbuilt stimuli responses—the bird making its nest; the squirrel laying by its store of nuts; the caterpillar weaving its cocoon; and so on endlessly. With rare enough exceptions, animals live in the world of immediacy. Until their days are over, it is always only today.

We have already suggested that many human beings live mainly in and by the day, referring particularly to the peasant and the casual laborer and, notably, the tramp or the hobo. There are of course the thrifty peasants who have some title or tenure over a small piece of land and are careful to save whatever they can, but there are also

65

the subsistence peasants who engage in unremitting toil merely to keep body and soul together, who have no prospect of a future, no horizon, who are dulled to thought and too weary for it at the day's end. For them the future is what happens to happen.

Even under better conditions there are people who live mostly by the day—until something shocks them with the menace of the future. When one's work is sufficiently a source of interest and self-esteem, this is perhaps as desirable a way to live as any, especially if thereby there is secured also some provision for the morrow. Certainly one cannot find enjoyment or any happiness except in the living present, even if part of one's present joy is remembrance of past achievement or anticipation of some coming boon. There is, for example, the craftsman or the technician who takes pleasure in his skill and has little ambition except to see the work grow under his hand. He may be the type of the village blacksmith of Longfellow, who is ready for the night's repose he has earned in the contentment of "something attempted, something done." And there are those who find in the domestic round and the evening's game or gossip enough to occupy their minds without the need for forethought or the spur of foreboding.

It is, on the other hand, the men of some affluence and status who are most likely to be preoccupied with the future. Property outlives the owner. He is concerned with its disposition after he is gone. Wealth breeds more wealth, but it increases or diminishes according to the forethought given to it. The future of others is linked to the life of the property owner. The linkage between time and money is so binding that the well-to-do can rarely escape the incessant question mark of the future. It is so no less with men of affairs generally, executives, officials, politicians. They must endeavor to meet the tides of events, to prepare ahead for contingencies. And if their rank is high enough, they participate in movements and policies that sweep on to destinies they will never live to share.

But this type of preoccupation is itself a protection against the brooding fears associated with growing older. The man of affairs is engrossed with the future of his business, with the course of events, with the activities of large institutions. He identifies his own future with the developments occurring in these institutions. He projects his own life into the continuity of their lives. Only when some too obvious evidence of his own mortality strikes him is he likely to be seriously concerned about it.

The more sophisticated and cultured members of the community, including the practitioners of the arts and sciences, have a somewhat different preoccupation with the future. They live in a rather more stable world than that of the men of affairs. While there is an ingredient of fashion in the arts and of new directions in the sciences, they are part of an enduring culture reaching back into the distant past. The old is not scrapped when new developments occur. These areas are mostly free from the hustling urgencies of the world of affairs. The people whom they attract are more reflective. Among them are those who "look before and after, and sigh for what is not." They have time to be concerned about the brevity of time and the paucity of achievement. They lack the protection of the men of affairs who ride forward on the urgencies of events. And when they do become successful enough to grow complacent, some disturbing thought of mortality is likely sooner or later to break in. Of them it can often enough be said:

> Just when we're safest, there's a sunset touch,
> A fancy from a flower-bell, some one's death,
> A chorus-ending from Euripides,
> And that's enough for fifty hopes and fears—
> The grand Perhaps.

Diverse are the responses men make to the unyielding disparity between the demand and the supply of time, but there are certain rather common expedients to mitigate the realization that the time remainder is inexorably decreasing. For example, when something reminds us that only a few years on we shall reach retirement age, we think of someone who remains an alert and highly efficient executive in his middle eighties. Or when we fear our physical powers may be declining, we recall someone who plays a respectable game of tennis in his late seventies. The example is set before us—we may have a long time yet to go. And who can say that the cherished hope for the longer prospect may not itself help to make it attainable? The belief is a special case of our tendency as we grow older to reassess the count whereat we regard youth as ended or middle age as ended, or at which we hold certain enjoyments or practices to be no longer appropriate—or perhaps feasible—for our advancing years. We may name this tendency—one that for both cultural and biological reasons is particularly noticeable in our own days—the *principle of the receding landmarks*.

There is another resort that has some affinity to it. The first applies to dates that are determined by a traditional reckoning unadapted to variations in vitality between individuals and under different conditions. No inexorable calendar says you are middle-aged at forty, but when you are forty, the count itself is ungainsayable. It is with birthdays and other anniversaries that the second principle has to do. You were still in your thirties until the calendar marked your fortieth birthday. Suddenly you seem to enter a new stage of life. You don't feel any different, any older, but your thirties are certainly past. You must get used to the fact that you are already in your forties. But you will be in your forties for what seems in prospect a very long time. After all, you're still pretty young in your forties, compared with the fifties or sixties or seventies. Possibly you may think that middle age begins at forty-five. Even so, you have several years before it comes. Till then the count has no finality. It is an indifferent interval. It lies between you and the next important reckoning with time. So again it happens in the fifties and in the sixties and onwards, as each new calendar adjustment is reached and passed.

We see the *principle of the indifferent interval* operating on a smaller scale in the course of the single year. Suppose we are fortunate enough to have, say, a month's vacation. When we begin to enjoy the country scene or the seaside breeze, we have an amplitude of time ahead. We can forget the duties and worries of office. It is, say, the beginning of August, and September is quite a long way off. But the last week comes, and as it wears on, we become more and more conscious that the days are numbered. The indifferent interval has vanished.

We may regard the belief in the indifferent interval as an illusion, and so from one aspect it is. For the pace of the years—*our* pace through the years—has no respite. Calendar-wise it moves as steadily when we are thirty-one as when we are thirty-nine. But from another aspect, a quite important aspect, the principle is valid enough. Once again we can appeal from clock time—or calendar time—to conscious time. We live in moments—the moments of consciousness, not of the clock—in continuities, in periods. And the indifferent interval is such a period, so long as we understand it is still a process, and not a halting place.

XIII

THE REACH INTO THE TIMELESS

Through the eternal we can conquer the future.
—SÖREN KIERKEGAARD

In various ways people have sought, and sometimes found, release from concern over the transience of life and the changefulness and disarray of earthly things. Leaving aside the recourse to distractions and indulgences and mere opiates that offer a fleeting escape into mental benumbedness and near oblivion, there is but one direction in which genuine liberation can be found. It is by dedication to a way of life so fulfilling to the personality or offering such promise of future fulfillment that the time is thereby "redeemed."

Several distinct approaches, all leading in this direction, are possible. One approach is through a wholehearted absorption in an interpersonal relationship so emotionally charged that it assumes a transcendent quality. The subject cannot conceive of any end to it or of a life that is not preoccupied with it. Another approach is through a consuming devotion to a nonpersonal interest or field of interest, one that offers ample opportunity for continuous exploration and stretches enticingly further the more it is explored. Yet another approach is found in full dedication to some conception of the divine or the eternal, the divine being or the eternal verity as intuited by or revealed to the believer.

The first approach requires of those who would follow it the capacity to find life satisfaction in the maintenance and development of a certain relationship to others. It may be a relationship to a whole group, say a passion for the liberty of a people or for service to the oppressed; it may be a wide humanitarian interest; or it may be a quite limited but intense concern for the welfare of a kin group or a particular brotherhood. On the other hand, it may be the passion of unicentered love, normally the love of man and woman. While many human beings fall under the spell of such passion for a period, the passionate element usually fades, even if the love endures. But to some the passion itself appears all-fulfilling, and when disillusionment succeeds, they are lost until another equally engrossing attachment takes its place. In an article on Brigitte Bardot the writer Simone de Beauvoir comments: "Brigitte confides to us, 'Every time I'm in love I think it's forever.' To dwell in eternity is one way of rejecting time."

The type of engrossment characterizing the second approach has a very different structure. The emotion that sustains it is steady and quiet, the emotion that accompanies an inexhaustible quest, an ongoing exploration calling for all the capacity of the devotee. We might regard Browning's grammarian as a literary exhibit of the type, the scholar who, borne by his disciples to the mountain top where he would breathe his last, already "dead from the waist down," kept on expounding to them the intricacies of the syntax of Ancient Greek. The example may be somewhat overcolored, but certainly there have been, and are today, scientists and other scholars so notably dedicated to their work that it has sufficed to fill the horizon of their thoughts and objectives. If not wholly, nevertheless essentially, such men "dwell in the eternity" of an ever present devotion. And this is true not by any means of scientists alone. Some artists have the temperament that can maintain this devotion. Almost any object of intrinsic interest, any cause, can become so all-engrossing to some receptive minds as to rule their thoughts and their dreams to the practical exclusion of all else. Any form of the collector's instinct, any hobby, any "movement" may suffice.

No mortal can be totally unmindful of the passing of the years; the signs are too manifest, within as well as without. And to be so greatly undisturbed by these reminders, as the dweller in eternity must be, demands something more than dedication to some unflagging interest. There must go with it a disposition that is indeed more rare. The intensity of an interest may otherwise actually evoke a constant apprehension about time. The contrast between the brevity of the time allotted and the ever receding horizons of the objective strikes home—and more nearly there is a task on the completion of which the heart is set and the bell may toll before it is accomplished. Life is always vital to those who want to work on.

What more is needed to blunt the edge of the encroaching end is, at the least, a constant sense of self-fulfillment within the work to which one is dedicated, such that it outweighs, among other things, the inroads of the years on one's personal relationships.

Finally, there is the one approach that actually promises a complete redemption from the burdens and problems of the time process. Many profess to follow it, but few enough follow through. It is a difficult way, even for those who are committed to seeking it. It is built on faith, an implicitly accepted religious creed. The faith is embodied in religions as diverse as those of Jesus and of Buddha. It affirms that this life is a transitional period to another mode of being where "there is no more time." The disciple, by following the prescribed way, makes the time process a preparation for eternity. The eternal reality, of which earthly existence is but the troubled shadow, awaits. In the Buddhistic form this reality is the self-obliterating nothingness of everlasting peace. In the Christian form it is the paradise of angels and of saints in the light of the presence of the eternal God.

By preparing steadfastly for this eternity, the faithful must attune themselves to dwelling in eternity while still sharing the life of mortality. The process of preparation in these two great faiths has common but also divergent features. Both have codes of ethics that prescribe regard for others, the brotherhood of man, self-sacrifice, meekness, purity and such like virtues. The Buddhist way, however, is more ascetic, more renunciatory of the whole competitive frame of ordinary life, on the whole more quiescent. The Christian way is more concerned with sin as guilt, for which repentance has to be made and remission obtained and the evil of which is so inborn in human nature and so overwhelming that only the extreme sacrificial offering of the God himself in the form of Christ sufficed to bring salvation to the world.

But the faithful do not win in this life the bliss of dwelling in eternity merely by following a system of moral principles. The way to that goal is opened by belief, belief in the transcendental or mystical element, the revelation that animates each creed. When this belief takes full hold of the mind and heart of the disciple, he learns to live in the spirit of it. He has reached out to the timeless. The Christian must go apart, even when he remains in the world. He must give himself to reverential contemplation and loving service, so that he lives in the beatific vision of God. Such is the way of the saints. The Buddhist must acquire complete detachment from material concerns and the pleasures of the senses, from the whole whirl of motion and of change, so that he becomes attuned to the final consummation of never being born again. Such is the way of the great mahatmas.

It would then appear that the attitude that can override

the commotions of change, the blows of time and circumstance and the fears that the approach of old age and death engender is the product of the fervent belief in a creed that makes belief itself the precondition of the timelessness for which mortals yearn. The belief induces the practice of the faith and the practice confirms the attitude congenial to the faith. In this sense the belief—when it is fervent enough—is self-fulfilling.

Herein may lie the difference between the conceptions of an eternally changeless reality entertained in various philosophical systems and the religious versions of timelessness. We have had occasion to refer to the Platonic notion of pure, eternal forms, the molds, so to speak, of which earthly sense objects are but imperfect casts or simulacra made of insubstantial material. In a somewhat similar vein the philosopher Spinoza, who was called a "God-intoxicated man," was fascinated by the eternal being of mathematical forms. But none of the idealistic philosophers held out to men the prospect of dwelling in eternity while yet they lived. The most that can be claimed is that the philosophic mind itself, with its contemplation of absolute being or eternal realities, may develop a standard of values that to some degree releases it from the turmoils and uncertainties of mortal life.

PART FOUR

What Stays, What Comes, What Goes

XIV

PERSONAL IDENTITY AND THE TIME BRACKET

Cut away the future, and the present collapses, emptied of its proper content. Immediate existence requires the insertion of the future in the crannies of the present.
—ALFRED NORTH WHITEHEAD,
Adventures of Ideas

IN WHAT SENSE does anything endure, stay the same through time? More particularly, how and in what sense do individuals maintain their personal identities in spite of the great changes they undergo as they pass from childhood to old age? Like every other created thing from wisps of cloud to galaxies, the organism fulfills its own inevitable process. The mind of man subtly suffers continuous change. Yet endurance is as predictable as change, and indeed we predicate change only for that which endures.

The human personality has its own unique way of enduring through change, its own way of preserving its identity and its *sense* of identity. To begin with, let us observe that while the organism suffers change, the mind also *experiences* change. The difference is primary.

The dramatic quality of life is made possible by the fact that the mind is able to bracket the past, the present and the future. It thus establishes a framework for identity through change that is utterly unknown where consciousness is entirely absent. Consciousness overrides the instantaneousness of the present. As we have pointed out, the moment of consciousness is itself a duration, embracing the receding edge of the passing along with the oncoming edge of the future.

Here we have the ground for the continuous sense of identity through time. A being that was aware only of the successive instants of a swiftly obliterated present could hardly attain the recognition of its selfhood. But creative mind, aware of its passage through time in the freedom of its ampler present, proceeds to build and protect its identity throughout the changes of the organism and of itself. The memory can thus reach into the remoter recesses of the past and link the recollection of this past to its projection of the future. New experience is assimilated to older experience. The personality thus ratifies its self-integrity.

But the recognition of one's selfhood would still remain partial and quite insecure were it not socially sustained. A man who is entirely cut off from all human associations is likely to become a victim of fantasies and at length to lose his mind altogether. In the recognition accorded by others and in the give and take of social dealings the individual personality is confirmed, stabilized and elicited. In our relations with others we realize the impact of our selfhood as it is reflected back from other minds. Just as if we never saw our mirror image, we would not know what our own faces were like, so without the mirror reflection of our personality in the responsiveness to it of others we would lack the dynamic appreciation of our own being. Moreover, reciprocity with other men makes us agents endowed with responsibility and thus gives us a determinate significance within our society.

No less important is the fact that these others are members with us of a common group, a community. The community is far more enduring than its individual members, and within its relative immortality the individual can find some assurance against the fragility of his private existence. That of which he is a part abides. He is moored in the continuity of that to which he belongs.

These then are the three ways in which personal identity is secured against the incessant processes of change within and without: first, through the time brackets the mind creates in the linkage of past, present and future; second, through the give and take of social interchange; third, through the anchorage of membership in the enduring community.

Group belongingness is the haven of personality, tempering in many ways the raw precariousness of existence in the natural world and guarding it against the mortal loneliness of a life that is destined to end in death. From birth to death human beings are wholly dependent on the presence and the interrelated activities of their fellows. And death itself is socialized by solemn rituals and the concerted insignia of mourning. Men seek to perpetuate the recognition of their being even after their decease. Portraits and other memorials are handed on. Every graveyard is filled with muted appeals for remembrance. Some peoples have carried this yearning to a pathological extreme, notably the ancient Egyptians, with their vast pyramids, their jeweled caskets and their mummies.

The creative artist strives toward immortality in a more meaningful way. His mission is to communicate in words, in paint, in metals, in stone, and when he succeeds, he impresses both his message and his personality—for the two are inseparable—on other men. If his communication is really significant, it is not for his contemporaries alone but also for later generations. So Horace said of his poems that he had "erected a monument more enduring than brass." And Shakespeare in his sonnets repeatedly dwells on the thought that these tributes—but, alas, to his unknown beloved—would immortalize their object. Of the immortality of his own work he was sufficiently assured.

> Nor shall Death brag thou wanderest in his
> shade,
> When in eternal lines to time thou growest.
> So long as men can breathe, or eyes can see,
> So long lives this, and this gives life to thee.

In passing we may note that this relative immortality of the creative product, or of the name and fame of its creator, has no relation to the continuance of personal identity, which is our main interest here. A man's deeds, for better or worse, may live after him. A man's thoughts and dreams, the intimate expressions of his personality, may survive to influence men of a later age. But the living cannot relate themselves to the being whose memory they may still cherish or he to them. Posthumous immortality is an insubstantial thing. The being to whom it is attributed has finished his work, communicates no more and is oblivious of the fame he enjoys.

Just as the individual asserts his identity throughout the incessant processes that carry him from youth to age, so the social group, the community, clings to its oneness throughout the gross vicissitudes of its history. Since the group endures though its members pass away, it has no necessary term to its existence. Even the family stakes its claim to identity over generations, sometimes over many generations. The name endures, the family tree is the branching of the stock; the inheritance of property, perhaps of an ancestral estate, is deemed a witness to its perpetuity; and for the more distinguished families a coat of arms and other insignia blazon their integrity throughout the generations. But what is thus taken for identity is no more than continuity, a continuity that grows ever thinner as the generations pass. Nature has decreed that only through intermixture can a new generation succeed the older. What is regarded as the original blood, the blood of a great-great-grandfather, say, itself the product of a myriad crosses, is merged with that of many others in those who claim descent from it. Every generation signifies an unpredictable new mixing of genes in the complex working of heredity.

When we turn to the larger social group, however, we find a stronger claim to continued identity. The biological stock of the relatively insulated group may not as a whole be much affected by the infusion of new blood over a few generations—though the innumerable chances of new hereditary combinations will always make each new generation somewhat different from any earlier one. Moreover, during any considerable stretch of time, there are likely to be migrations of various sorts, raids and invasions and other sources of intermixtures. The sense of identity need not be affected, because it is sustained by the folkways, the cultural patterning into which each new generation is adapted. For the greater societies it is the culture rather than the presumptive blood bond that makes the folk one through time, a community with a history of its own, codes of its own and a sense of its own peculiar quality. Common interests, modes of speech, a network of interrelationships and a homeland reinforce the solidarity of the folk. It is strongest and most enduring when it achieves the form of nationhood.

Nevertheless, even for the nation its presumptive identity through time is primarily a culturally sustained belief in identity, a solidarity of the people that proclaims their continuous oneness. Within a few generations the culture, the attitudes, the beliefs, the ways of living, the aspirations of a people undergo so many changes that were a present member transported back through these generations, he would seem to be among an alien folk. But since there is no break in the historical solidarity, the belief in oneness withstands all the impacts of change.

Anchored in the assurance of the immortality of the community and sustained by the beliefs and traditions of its culture, the individual members share an inner environment that blankets them, in whatever measure, against the brute design of organic nature and thus helps to protect the sense of personal identity through the flux of the changeful years.

XV
HISTORY AS THE TEST OF TIME

> *Tout passe—l'art robuste*
> *Seul a l'eternité;*
> *Le buste*
> *Survit à la cité.*

—THÉOPHILE GAUTIER, *L'Art*

THE DEEDS of men sink into the melting pot of time, with countless ripples that quickly disappear. Fathers beget children whose deeds have like small repercussions and so from generation to generation. Some few make a deeper impression on the surface of their age, mostly by unloosing deeds of violence—wars and conquests and revolutions—that devastate the lives and homes of ordinary folk. But new generations arise and new beginnings are made, and the record of these deeds becomes the dim memory of an alien time. Rarely there is the kind of upheaval that shakes and seems to change the course of history, and the zealots proclaim that the world's great age begins anew. The French Revolution was such, but its hopes of liberty, equality and fraternity were drowned in terror and dictatorship. The Soviet Revolution was a political earthquake of quite unusual magnitude, but again the utopia of classless freedom it promised soon proved the reign of a new monolithic power. Perhaps what these great social upheavals do is to burst the shell of a decaying social order that otherwise would have slowly crumbled before the continuous thrusts of deep-working trends. Their very violence, how-

81

ever, distorts the operation of these trends, and we may surmise that in the longer perspective the great revolutions are but episodes, at best precipitants of the long-term processes that determine the course of human history.

Whatever happens, whatever is accomplished has some impact, however small, on other things, in some degree affects the way some other things happen. Every thread of causation weaves into the vast continuous chain of history. Most of the things men do, however, live on only in the thin sense that they conspire with other doings to change in some manner some things that happen later, nobody knows how much or how far.

If, however, we want to know what things that men do actually live on, live on in their own right, so to speak —live on in their own integrity—we must look elsewhere than to the deeds of the mighty. Even the bones of the dead, as Sir Thomas Browne put it, outlast "the drums and tramplings of three conquests." The small land of Palestine was conquered by the Romans and its holy places sacked, but the religion it gave the world lived on, and the religion that was born of the former conquered the conquerors. The temples of ancient Athens were overthrown and the city-state that erected them has long been obsolete, but the culture the city-state developed—its drama, scripture, poetry, philosophy—lives on and still fires the imagination of men. Therein is the heritage of time, the triumph of man's spirit over the eroding forces of the material cosmos.

It is the products of the creative mind that alone have the potentiality of enduring intact through all the changes of human history and of the environmental conditions under which man lives. This creative activity has two directions. One is, broadly speaking, utilitarian; the development and application of the skills that increase productivity and provide us with more of the necessities and all of the comforts and luxuries we enjoy, the skills that have brought mankind from the mud hut and the cave to the towers and spires of the modern city; the inventive ingenuity that has given us IBM machines and sound out-distancing planes and tractors and atomic reactors.

The other is, again broadly speaking, culture. The products of the first direction are primarily means, devices and instruments that enable men to live more abundantly, to enjoy more comforts, to travel with greater ease and greater speed—in general, to accomplish their objectives, whatever they may be, more fully than before. The products of the second direction are primarily valued for themselves, not in the first instance because they serve other ends. We read a colorful story or go to see a play because we are interested in it. We take part in amateur games or sports because we enjoy them. We worship—if we really worship—because we find solace or inspiration in so doing. We listen to music and have regard for works of art and high design because we appreciate these things. To this area belongs the whole range of what we have ventured to call myths.

We use the word *myth* here in a special sense, congenial to its original meaning, since we have no more appropriate term. In this reference the word conveys no suggestion whatever of falsity. Any mode in which men express some idea about the nature of things, about the way things happen or their own relations to events—in more technical language, any conceptual structure—is in this reference a myth. Creed, doctrine, parable, folklore, philosophy, theory are equally within the category. Man never grasps the whole significance, the whole truth, about anything. But however much or however little he knows, the untutored savage and the greatest sage alike have their conceptions about the near and the farther world and about their place in it. One difference is that the sage is acutely aware how partial, fragmentary, hypothetical, imperfect his knowledge is. Our words are signs that identify things, symbols that represent our impressions of things, tools to help us to organize and manipulate things. But what these words convey is at best only the glimpses our senses, aided by instruments of precision, can reach and our reason can infer. We interpret these glimpses; we systematize them as best we can. So we construct *our* reality, the human adumbration of the reality that lies back of the glimpses.

The distinction between these two orders of creative product, between the technological device and, say, the drama or the painting or the doctrine, is far from being absolute. Products of the first order may embody cultural values and products of the second order may have practical utility as means. Some products in architecture, for example, are at once utilitarian and cultural, so built as to be at once artistic, endowed with beauty of line and of proportion and also serviceable as dwelling places. But by and large the distinction holds between objects and services that are primarily utilitarian, like automobiles, garages, government offices and factories, and those that are in the first instance values in themselves, appreciated for their own sake and not merely or mainly for some further use we can make of them, like objects of art, music, worship, thoughts that live with us.

The distinction is manifested in the difference between the way these two modes of human creation live in history. Take a machine as an example of the first order. Any given type of machine is rapidly superseded by one that in some respect is more efficient, and it in turn is likely to be finally outmoded by a new type altogether. Obsolescence is a process that occurs over the whole range of industrial activity. While it may require a genius to invent a new mechanical contrivance, say the steam engine or the turbine, lesser ingenuity can find ways of improving it and in time transforming its character. The model of this year is soon outmoded by a superior model.

The original embodiment of invention is soon obsolete, but the invention itself initiated an endless chain of progressively more efficient mechanisms. In this sense it lives on in history and has a cumulative impact on the habits and ways of men. The invention, the new mechanism, sets in motion a series of developments that has no necessary end. The original mechanism may become a museum piece, like an early steam engine, or be lost in the depths of antiquity, like the first specimens of the wheel, but ever afterward the history of mankind is increasingly affected by the evolution of the invention. Nowhere else in the affairs of men can progress be so confidently predicted as it can in this world of technology. Not infrequently, indeed, we delude ourselves into thinking that the advance of technology—the evidences of greater productivity, greater power at our command, greater speed and so forth—suffices to establish social progress.

The machine must quickly grow obsolete, but the cultural product, the myth, call it what you will, is subject to no such imperative. While its significance will change, its vitality, its original form may endure through centuries and even through millenniums. If the material in which the conception is embodied is stone or metal or pigment on some kind of surface, it must of course suffer the fate of all material constructs, but even so the conception itself can be re-embodied or reproduced so that its main significance is perpetuated. If the conception is embodied in some symbolic form, in words, designs, or mathematical equations, it is potentially immortal so long as men have eyes to see and minds to comprehend. The Homeric poems are some twenty-five hundred years old, and a few scholars still enjoy them in the original tongue, while considerable numbers read them in one translation or another. The Bible is translated into practically every language in the world. All the great religions carry their original message to multitudes over all the centuries. The great literature of the past, in philosophy, poetry, drama and story, not only lives on but, because of the development of the media of communication, is appreciated over a wider range of the earth than ever before.

These creations of the human mind become a treasure house from which later generations continually draw. They undergo change not in themselves but mostly in the form of reinterpretation to suit new insights, new conditions and new needs. Thus they selectively live on without any necessary loss of vitality. The greater doctrines, the greater myths are flexible as well as universal in their appeal, for they enshrine concepts of grandeur, of beauty, intimations concerning the lot and the destiny of man, manifestations of significant form, perspectives on man's relation to the universe.

Such creations, as the saying goes, stand the test of time in a way that no other work of man can achieve. Empires rise and fall; civilizations flourish and decay; revolutions erupt and settle down; styles and fashions come and go, while these creations alone retain their surpassing integrity. They are the part of history that endures through history.

What then is it that possesses such vitality? It is the product of the free creativeness of the mind, the symbolic expression of insight and experience. It lives on when and because the communication is intrinsically significant, wholly individualized and yet responding to the deeper common needs or aspirations of men, or stirring the fountains of emotion, or throwing some glimpse of light on the greater problems of human relationships. The work that lives may be a heroic tale with the splendor of style, like Homer's *Iliad,* or a probing discourse on the government of man, like Plato's *Republic,* or a drama presenting the clash between the strength and the weakness of the great like *Oedipus Rex* or *Hamlet,* or a vision of beauty, like the poetry of Keats. The gross satirist, like Rabelais, and the magistral theologian, like Aquinas, may alike qualify. The simple tinker, like Bunyan, and the sophisticated aristocrat, like Montaigne, may equally win this crown of time.

The ground of this immortality is a way of thinking, an imaginative projection that may range from a formulation of the highest scientific abstractness to the portrayal of the lowest depths of human existence. The test of time vindicates the primacy of this greatness, conferring quality. It is the one attribute of mankind that, whatever others may be conjoined with it, can endow a man's work with the power to live through the ages, so that long after his bones have turned to dust he still speaks to far-off generations.

To sum up the argument, the two forces that shape the longer course of history far more powerfully and enduringly than the violence of conquest and the exploits of men of affairs are the ingenuity that is embodied in the advance of technology and the imaginative thinking that has built up the great cultural heritage of mankind. The former changes the face of the earth, imposes on it the new environment that erupts everywhere into populous cities, with their towers and their factory chimneys, and turns the desert into irrigated fields. The second evokes, sustains and renews the aspirations, the traditions, the doctrines, the vital arts and the styles of living of the peoples, the dynamic purposes that express themselves in the consensus and clash of social enterprise. These two forces, the two creative directions of the mind, constitute the warp and the woof of the web of history, whereas the events of the history books, wars and commotions and the exploits of the great, are in this longer reach but passing and often disruptive episodes, the work of man's power and pride that break against the insistence of deeper working currents. The metaphor of warp and woof, however, does not convey the dynamic relationship between these two forces, since they are not only interwoven but also continuously interactive.

Human history, then, is not to be thought of as the narrative of a dead past, of a continuous series of pasts that died in giving birth to each successive present. It is so much more than a string of events; it is essentially the record of how two great operative principles surmounted environmental resistance and the destructive passions of men to build the precarious balance of civilization.

One of the two, the technological principle with its broadening scientific base is cumulatively progressive, allowing for occasional major catastrophes. Each technical advance makes others easier and is a step in the development of a more fully integrated system of technology. It is never, or most rarely, reversed, and it is outmoded only by new advances based on it. Once achieved, it spreads in time from people to people, so that at length a single system of technology is common to mankind.

The other principle, creative culture, has no such assured thrust into the future. Its achievements, on the other hand, are never wholly outmoded, and some of them are unique in that they are carried in their original integrity through eras of time. But what they communicate cannot be transmitted or enjoyed in the facile way in which technological achievement can be utilized. They are communicable only to those who can appreciate the communication. In this great area, therefore, there is no guarantee of progress from generation to generation. The cultural progress of generation after generation is hard to assess and, however assessed, can never be predicted. Instead of the upward line of technological advance, we have more or less sporadic ups and downs. In the arts, in the spiritual and religious realm, in the standards of popular culture, in the morale of the times, history offers no guarantee whatever of continuous progress.

XVI
BEGINNINGS

You cannot step twice into the same river, for new water is always flowing in.—HERACLITUS

ALL COMPOSITE THINGS begin at a time, endure for a time, change in time and end at a time. Unless we accept these premises, all change becomes wholly unintelligible. It would follow that so long as anything happens or begins in the wide universe, so long as there is a universe—or the creator of a universe—time must already exist. Time itself then can have no beginning.

In the beginning was hydrogen; in the beginning was God; in the beginning was the word. We inquire and surmise and speculate about beginnings, but always it turns out to be about some primal element, some archetype, some potency, some first mover, and always it begs the question: What was before the first, and how did the first come to be? If out of nothingness nothing comes, then there was no "first" that was not always; then there was no absolute beginning, and there can be no absolute end.

The notion that there can be creation out of nothing is an old one. It seems to be implied in certain theological doctrines to the effect that God created the world by mere fiat. It is also assumed, within limits, in the notion of spontaneous generation. It is wholly at odds with the scientific approach, although one modern astrophysicist has propounded a theory that the universe is maintained in a steady state by the creation—out of nothing—of a new atom of hydrogen once in a while.

The universe is full of new beginnings. All the formations we know of, planets and stars and plants and men, have come to be what they now are. But none of these forms of being were sudden creations. There are sudden endings, the breakup all at once of great constructions that took centuries or eons to build. A hydrogen bomb destroys in an instant a great city with all that inhabit it and all the heritage of ages it contains. A supernova, which to our remote eyes appears as a sudden new spot of brightness somewhere among the myriad lights of the night sky, is a stupendously vaster cataclysm, the explosion not simply of a star but of members of two colliding systems. There are, however, no comparable sudden beginnings, save for the dissolution products of a sudden ending.

The universe constantly gestates new beginnings. All things change, expand, contract, lose or gain materials, increase or decrease their radiant energies, enter into new contacts, new relationships. Mostly these new beginnings are modifications of a previous state, aspects of an order already known and capable of being predicted if the previous state is known. There is, however, one kind of new beginning that is beyond the range of prediction, a kind that raises some most intriguing questions. Such beginnings emerge in the course of evolutionary change. The evolution of life is the one clear example of evolution we know, in the full significance of that term. Through the ages life has moved through a series of stages, from unicellular forms through to the higher mammals and man. Here our question can be sharpened. Is the line so continuous that there are no new directions but only the fuller emergence of characters and attributes that were latent before? Was the potency of man already in the amoeba? If so, in what sense?

Man, the present apex of the evolutionary thrust, has many attributes of which there is not the remotest suggestion on the level of the unicellular mite. Between his appearance and theirs numerous very significant new beginnings must have happened in the biological line. How they came to be is a question the present writer believes is far from being explained. Continuity that exhibits such remarkable changes is far more than mere continuity, nor does the resort to the principles of adaptation to environment and natural selection seem sufficient to explain the *direction* of evolution, which has successively exhibited new and more complex and more gifted forms of life.

An even more crucial question concerning continuity and beginnings lies in the emergence of life itself. In the first place the chemistry of life is organic, and the chemistry of the material world is inorganic, except that under very special conditions, which the earth may have somewhere offered at some stage of its development, organic compounds can form from the inorganic. Experiment has shown that electric currents simulating lightning can evoke in a suitable medium the production of proteins. When a conjuncture of conditions produced the first natural proteins, there and then was a beginning of commanding importance for us, since proteins are the building blocks of organism.

But the major question remains. The line from the inorganic to the organic is continuous. The line therefore from the nonliving to the living is continuous and among the living from the simplest forms of vegetative existence to the highest exhibit of the animal world. Along this line the appearance of proteins was a new beginning. But what of life itself, that cunningly utilizes these proteins to initiate and to perpetuate an entirely new way of existing? The beginning of life was the beginning of a tremendous series of new beginnings that brought to earth mosses and ferns and flowering trees, Crustacea and Mollusca and reptiles and birds and mammals and man. It is surely little enough to say that the first replicating protein units, the first germ cells, were the greatest of all beginnings.

Moreover, life has been continuous in a way that is all its own. Life reproduces; germ cells pass from parents to offspring. While billions of germ cells perish all the time, enough fulfill the function of reproduction to assure the continuation of the species. Thus the germ plasm lives on through countless generations. The chain of life is continuous because the germ plasm endures.

In an earlier chapter we ventured the assertion that whatever begins must also end. Here it may seem a contradiction to assert that some beginnings do not necessarily imply an ending. Life is capable of reproducing itself wherever and so long as there is a favorable environment. Some far-off day our planet is destined to become inhospitable to any life, as it was when the planet first went spinning as a fiery ball. But it is not inconceivable that before that distant date man will have learned to migrate to another planet, which and where none can now surmise. However, even if life should perish on the earth, it seems most probable that somewhere else life perpetuates itself, perhaps in millions and millions of the planets around other suns.

Life, then, is potentially immortal, if we can assume that always among the countless suns there will be somewhere the conditions congenial to its existence. Life had its beginning on our earth when these conditions appeared. Life needed these conditions to manifest itself. But life is not its conditions. We need certain conditions in order that electricity may produce a spark or become a current. But electricity is not its conditions—it is inherent in the very nature of the universe. It would be very rash to assume that life itself began when our own little planet was ready for it. Life need not be the child of time.

If this argument should seem speculative, let us note

there is another sense in which life exhibits a remarkable resistance to time or, more strictly, to the normal processes that other forms of activity undergo in the course of time. We have referred to life as a potency, an energy that comes into play under certain conditions. But it seems to behave differently from the great energy principles of the inanimate world. These other energies, all the forms and expressions of radiant energy, tend to diminish or dissipate themselves or to be transformed into diffused heat. The life energy, operating through reproduction and variation and mutation, is inherently expansive. Life has the urge to multiply, and in the process of evolution it moves on from the simplest expressions to others so complex and so elaborately functional that biochemists are not likely even in long ages to comprehend fully the manner in which they operate or to explain why they are capable of so operating. Life reveals itself thus as an endless system of new beginnings.

And beginnings of this nature have a special dramatic quality. They not only make manifest characters that were merely hinted at in earlier forms, they not only give new range to tendencies more limited before, they also reveal new directions, new avenues hitherto unopened. Imagine a present-day scientist, or yourself in that role, transported back in a time machine to the age of the first algae and bacteria. How impossible it would have been to predict the age of the fishes and the frogs or, in that age again, to predict the age of the dinosaurs or in that age to surmise the coming of the primates or then of man. The course of evolution is rife with unheralded new beginnings. And since life has been on this earth only some two billion years, and it has probably billions of years still to go, who can deny that countless more new life beginnings may yet lie ahead upon it?

XVII

BEGINNINGS—AND ENDINGS

Time hath, my lord, a wallet at his back
Wherein he puts alms for oblivion.
—WILLIAM SHAKESPEARE, *Troilus and Cressida*

ALL EXISTENCE for all creation—for all but the primary infinitesimals and the primary energies, the uncompounded universals—is a process that lies between a beginning and an end, between that which is not yet and that which is no more.

We take this simple statement for granted, but when we seek to apply it, we run into problems. Wherever there is energy, there is change. Something is different from what it was before. Thus something new, the change, comes into being. Nothing comes out of nothing. The new beginning is itself prepared for by what was before. It is not an absolute beginning. No Aphrodite comes all at once from out of the sea. No first Adam was ever created by decree. What we call the beginning has claims on the past, and what we call the end has claims on the future.

Let us consider what this means. Let us take, for example, some human artifact, say a violin. Let us suppose it was made in the year 1860 and destroyed by a bomb in 1943. It did not all at once come into existence. The craftsman worked on it for many months. It became a violin, shall we say, when the last string was pegged. It was some time in the making, though it was destroyed

in an instant. The discrepancy between the travail of creation and the swift casualness of destruction is a common
enough difference between beginnings and endings.

The contrast here displayed between the making and
the ending has much deeper implications. When did the
violin begin to be a violin? That is one of those logical
problems you can answer as you please. But did the violin
really begin to be made when the craftsman started his
operation? He couldn't have started on it unless he had in
mind the idea of a violin, the fore-image of the finished
work. This image was itself the product of a long process
of evolution of stringed instruments, reaching back to the
forgotten age when someone first noticed that a taut
fiber plucked by a finger gave out a particular resonance.
The beginnings of the violin thus carry us back through
all the ages. A particular violin may be dated, say from
1860, but the preparation for it began in the distant past.

That is what we mean by saying that beginnings have
a claim on the past. What makes them possible is a whole
series of prior beginnings. What is true of the beginnings
of artifacts or constructed objects of any kind is true also
of the beginnings of particular organisms—with a difference. In the former case there is the evolution of the form,
which is copied, as it were, with variations in a series of
successive instruments. In the latter case there is also the
evolution of a form, or rather of a great array of diverg-
ing forms that branch off from some early or rudimentary
form, ramifying into species and genera and families and
orders. The form, the type, endures through ages. The
type of which all plants are differential expressions and
the type of which all animals are derivations stem back to
some elementary type that was not explicitly either vegetative or animal but perhaps an undifferentiated precursor
of both. In any event it is obvious that the type forms of
all things, whether organisms or constructs, are strongly
persistent through time and maintain a system of order

throughout the endless transience of the things themselves. This reflection lies back of the Platonic doctrine which asserted that the types, the ideas imperfectly realized in objects, are themselves the ultimate realities, pure and timeless.

There is, however, a very significant difference between the modes in which organic types and the types of artifacts respectively persist. The latter are culturally transmitted, conveyed in the lore of the successive generations as they become acquainted with the objects themselves and learn the techniques involved in their construction. The former are biologically transmitted in the continuity of the germ plasm as it passes to offspring from parents.

We must, then, be on our guard when we speak of beginnings. There are no absolute beginnings, no points in time to which we can assign the first step in the making of things. Consider our violin—it had various antecedents receding deep into the past, and these had antecedents in turn. At length, probably not before the fifteenth century, there was developed from these antecedents the distinctive instrument we call the violin. The violin-maker learns the design before he takes up his trade. Thus even the particular instrument he is making has its beginnings long before he sets to work on it.

We can of course say that the violin as we know it first appeared in the fifteenth century. That, however, is a relative beginning. We say a child was born on a certain day, conceived at a particular date. We have again significant beginnings, but still relative. The germ plasm that mingled at his conception traces back through a dateless heredity.

Endings, on the other hand, are often enough datable. Endings are often more conspicuous, more drastic, more historic than beginnings. They are the landmarks of the time schedule. Beginnings, even relative beginnings, may have a far greater significance—the course of the future is shaped by them—but the record makes much more note of endings. It learns of beginnings, if it ever does, belatedly. The birth of an empire may be obscure, but the fall of an empire resounds in the calendar. The unknown moment when life appeared on this earth inaugurated the tremendous process of evolution of which man is at present the climactic expression.

Endings exhibit a variety of modes according to the character of that which ceases to be. A physical object goes out of existence when it is broken up so as to lose its determinant features or when it is consumed or dissolved into its constituents. A physical process, say the emission of light from a star or the orbiting of a satellite round the earth, ends when the energy requisite for the process is exhausted or when it is converted into some other form of expression. A mechanical process ends when the mechanism is disrupted in any of various ways. An organizational activity ends when its objective is achieved or when it proves abortive or unsuccessful or when a change of policy or program cuts it short. A social organization may perish when its membership dwindles away or when it suffers bankruptcy or some kind of defeat or possibly when the purpose for which it was established is attained, say the passage of a particular law. (We say "possibly," because organizations have a tendency to outlive their usefulness and generally have a way of clinging to existence without too much regard for the need for them.)

Death is an ending that is quite unlike any of these other endings. It has many unique features. It is irremediable. When other objects cease to exist, there are actual or potential ways in which they can be restored, rebuilt or reactivated. The most seriously damaged machine can be reconstructed. The physical object that is shattered to fragments can be put together again. The defunct organization can be given a new lease on life.

But the dead organism cannot be revived. Objects that have used up their supply of energy can, under certain conditions, be provided with new energy stores. The energy, however, that animated the once dead body cannot be replaced. Once the heart stops beating for a relatively brief period, no power, no recourse can bring the organism back to life. This fact is closely associated with another. The body is composed of living cells that immediately begin to decay and disintegrate when death occurs. The life that animated the system maintains and renews every part, every constituent of the whole. The body and the life energy that animates it are integrally one, and as soon as the breath of life ceases, the whole system begins to decompose.

The ending that is death is brought about in hundreds of different ways. Life is at every stage exposed to threats and is constantly warding off one peril or another. A seemingly slight disturbance of the system, a small change in the chemistry of the body, the attack of any of thousands of viruses and bacteria, may be as fatal as the most violent shock. Life is upheld by a most cunningly adapted union of an elaborate system of psychical, chemical and physical forces.

The differences we have thus far cited between death and all other endings are, however, only the concomitants and conditions of more far-reaching differences. Death plays a profound role both in the evolutionary process and in the way that life is lived. Without death there would be neither sex nor reproduction, no fatherhood or motherhood, no growing up, no maturation, no urgent call for love or intimacy or warm desire, and little enough of the strivings and ambitions and of the natural groupings that are the prime bonds of any society. For were there no death, there would be no need for reproduction. If there were reproduction without mortality, it would soon become an insurmountable barrier to any kind of existence;

it would somehow have to be prevented, and thus the potentiality of reproduction would atrophy.

Without death, therefore, there would be no renewal in the world of life, no surge of disturbing energies, no fresh approaches to old problems, no new goals. Without reproduction there could be no evolution of life, no ascent up which life could climb to greater heights. We know enough concerning the conditions under which life began to realize that very lowly forms of life must precede and prepare the way for higher forms. Reproduction means variation and gives opportunity for the fuller expression of life's potentialities as the generations succeed one another and new species emerge in the succession. Reproduction is thus the ground for trial and error, for experimentation, for the whole great enterprise that fills the land and the sea with myriad kinds of living things and also for the multitude of special exhibits of that enterprise that are initiated by the restlessly probing spirit of man. Without death the great evolutionary adventure could never have begun, and life itself would have remained unrevealed.

Even if by some miracle man could have appeared with all his latent capacities, but in a world in which there was no death, it is scarcely credible that these capacities could have attained any high development. Why should anyone seek to redeem the time when time can be no threat? Why should there be any urgency to achieve when there is an ocean of time ahead? What significance could there be in action were there an endless future in which to act?

In such a world nothing would be irremediable, nothing would have great consequence for the future, since the future in its unendingness has no concern for what the moment does. There could be no decisiveness in action, no finality. Without the danger of death, what would happen to heroism and to great adventure? No tragedy would impend, and no depths of emotion could be reached.

Life would be lived at best on a level of cool tranquility, undisturbed by changing demands of changing times. There would be no sting in experience and no excitement in new discovery.

In such a world what place could there be for passion or pity, for sympathy or fear, pathos or sorrow? Beings that know not death must find their satisfaction in the contemplation of the eternal verities. But while no doubt this type of contemplation has been the goal of our metaphysicians and of our saints, in itself alone, apart from the emotional experiences of this earthly life, such contemplation would surely be denuded of all the qualities that make us human. As one forgotten but delightful poet, William Johnson Cory, put it:

> Forsooth the present we must give
> To that which cannot pass away;
> All beauteous things for which we live
> By laws of time and space decay.
> But oh, the very reason why
> I clasp them, is because they die.

Here then is an ending unlike any other, one that in the intricate involvement of natural agencies is the condition of countless new beginnings, while it endows the life it destroys with unending potentialities of new and fuller living. Should we not add that death is a condition also of the only kind of immortality we actually know, the continuity and renewal of life in the succession of the generations, a process that need never cease so long as throughout the infinitude of space there exists one little world favorable to its existence?

For the living themselves, beyond all the fears the thought of death inspires, the cutting short of all they still would live for, there remains the consolation of an ending that is surcease from pain and puts the quietus on

all their troubles. So it is frequently conceived of as the
final homecoming, the settlement of all accounts—"Home
art gone and ta'en thy wages"—or the port after stormy
seas in which all voyaging ends.

PART FIVE

Approach to the Deeper Problems of Time

XVIII
TIME AND HISTORICAL REALITY

> *The future belongs to the essence of present fact and has no actuality other than the actuality of present fact.*
>
> —ALFRED NORTH WHITEHEAD,
> *Adventures of Ideas*

IN THE following two chapters we skirt the edge of the great unknown, the fundamental questions concerning the character of time with which philosophers have struggled without, however, reducing the size of the question marks. Language has this dangerous advantage, that it gives us names for postulated realities so that we can speak about them as if we had some knowledge of them, although their meaning or their reality wholly eludes our grasp. It is well that when we reflect on time we should be aware that its role in the endless work of creation, its relation to the timeless realities, its infinitude, the very sense in which it is real at all, are problems with which the human mind has not succeeded in coping and which possibly it may not be qualified to solve. We shall not recount the attempts some philosophers have made to climb these heights. We shall be remaining in the foothills far below. Even so we shall be traveling over more difficult ground than before.

The past is no more; the future is not yet. It might seem to follow that the only reality in an ever-changing universe is that which exists in the *now,* the now that is already past before the word can be uttered. On this reckoning the universe becomes an infinite series of infinitesimal staccatos of existence, a weird succession of moments of being that have nevertheless no interval of nonbeing between them.

We have already disowned this nightmare logic. Whatever reality we can conceive, it is a continuity in which change takes place. If we think of time as a dimension through which everything moves—rather than as a force that moves everything resistlessly on—then it becomes easier to appreciate the substantive existence of reality with all its processes of change. For it is not timing but the processes inherent in created things to which we must attribute all change. Then also time becomes the proper correlative of space, and there are two interdependent frames within which all things move, the frame of space and the frame of time.

At any time and through all time physical reality is constituted thus:

1. The eternal energies and the elemental units that have an equivalence with these energies—the timeless realities;

2. The relatively enduring existences and the processes they are undergoing—the historical realities;

3. The system of relationships within which these two categories are bound by the laws of their being.

Otherwise stated, reality at every moment is that which endures beyond change, that which endures through change and that which is then passing away by reason of change, together forming an eternal order with its constitutive laws.

✓Time, then, is the cosmic dimension in which the endless variety of the eternal reality actualizes itself in the phases between creation and dissolution. Time is also the dimension in which the strangely endowed energy we call life develops in experience.

The present is the current stage of all processing. In the present some aspect of the real is individualized, some latency is unfolded, some potency is actualized. The amplitude of the present in which this stage is consummated may be a moment, a season or an epoch.

The present would itself not be real, would be merely a phantom appearance if it did not demand and embrace both its past and its future. A world outside of time would be a world of impotence, for potency expresses itself in action, and action is change. A timeless world would be a characterless world, for character must express itself, and its expression means change. A timeless world, in short, is meaningless.

The present state of all processes is the realization of what the past has through all ages been leading up to, been ripening for actualization. And in turn the present could not show what it has in it, what makes it different from the past, were there no future to show it in. The present drives into the future because of what it has in it to become. Frequently enough, in our own little mundane affairs, our later reflection tells us that this or that development was bound to happen, that we might have known the affair would end that way, that we should have foreseen this or that policy was leading up to trouble. In a far wider sense the present is the hindsight of history.

All situations, all systems, all existences save the uncreated eternals are working out what they had it in them to become, exposing afresh their properties as they react or respond to probing conditions, revealing even in their decay and dissolution the successive aspects of the particular existences they respectively possess. In like manner the history of humanity, and of all its divisions, has been the evocation thus far of the capacities, of the skills and the devices, of the thoughts and the emotions, of the desires and the schemes of human beings as they worked out for their well-being or their misery under the stresses and opportunities of every changing situation. The processes of the life energy seem curiously different, unforeseeable and adventurous by comparison with the operations of other energies. In the physical realm we can more or less predict the stages of an existence, say of a star or a galaxy, that are yet to come, but in the biological realm we have no grounds for inferring what stages may lie ahead.

No reality can be manifested at any one time; it requires a process in which its latent attributes respectively find expression. It needs a time span sufficient for it to pass through all its stages. We may conjecture that the whole cycle of structure formation and resolution repeats itself and repeats itself again through the infinitude of time. Then it is always true that the world's great age begins anew. Within the nearer reality known to us there are various cycles of more modest amplitude, the seasonal succession; the sequence of seed to fruit that is again the seed; the nebula that becomes the star that passes from blue to red and may yet perhaps give its dust to a new nebula, suggesting vast cosmic processes through beginnings to endings and new beginnings.

Cosmic history—so at least we must assume—fulfills its endless processing in accordance with laws that are eternally operative, each successive stage being the necessary sequel of the stage before. When we turn to human history, though its scale is utterly insignificant in the cosmic frame, we obtain a close-up of how the future is made in the present in ways that may be partly predictable and in ways that no knowledge of the past enables us to predict.

We may distinguish two ways in which man becomes a part author of his own history. In the first place human societies inherit cumulatively and selectively from past experience a culture, a lore, a body of traditions and usages that serve as a controlling and directing force and are strong safeguards against serious deviations from the established order. Should that order itself be overthrown in a time of grievous stress and social upheaval, the new controls build up another system of beliefs and usages, inevitably incorporating much of the old in the new. This heritage is the conservative force in human history. On the other hand, since new conditions continuously pose new problems and since new generations are rarely content to follow without deviation the established ways, there is a drive, open or covert, to develop new programs in the face of old discontents and new issues. This is the innovating force.

Since every society has a policy-making system, it endeavors to regulate and to plan for its future. Broadly speaking, we may regard the direction thus set as usually a diagonal between the impacts of the conservative and the innovating forces. Sometimes one gains the ascendant, sometimes the other, and there is always turmoil between them.

Thus man makes, in a measure that increases with his controls over nature, his own history. No doubt he fails frequently in his attempts to make the changed reality conform to his intentions. The results of his planning are often different from his anticipations, because his knowledge of the situation he deals with is always imperfect. He is, moreover, thwarted in another respect. No council of man plans the future of mankind, nor is there effective accord between great nations and great systems in the pursuit of objectives. The many minds of many men, the conflicts of interests between groups and the competitive or antagonistic designs of nations bring to naught much of our programming for the future. Were men wiser or more unselfish—perhaps the two conditions are one—they would be rather more successful history-makers.

Much of man's actual history-making expresses his doing but not his willing, since through ignorance, misunderstanding and the crossing of purposes, the harvest of his multifarious actions, whether designed to affect the future or merely to achieve some immediate aim, is a very different crop from that he wanted to produce. His very ingenuity may turn to his defeat, as when he harnesses instruments of great power only to bring dreadful perils upon himself. Human history has two aspects that in the past have moved on concurrently; on the one hand there is a record of the advancing arts, which enrich the life of man and also give him resources to satisfy increasingly his numerous wants, and, on the other, a record of blunders and credulities and the disastrous clashes of shortsighted ambitions, mitigated at intervals by the constructive planning of leaders with vision.

One reason why man's efforts to shape the future are so often futile or worse is that he is slow to learn the lessons of his own past. Some of the traditions he accumulates are out of accord with his evolving needs but persist in spite of their unfitness for new situations. When, for example, the handwriting was already on the wall, clearly intimating that the age of colonial rule was ending, the majority of imperial states were unwilling to come to terms with necessity and change subjection into alliance, engaging instead in costly strife that often destroyed all hope of a new adjustment.

In the planning of their future, men certainly must use

the experience of history. But history bequeaths to us so poor a record of its own reality. What passes for history is so sketchy, so partial, so dependent on the caprice and interest and prejudice and low vantage point of the recorders that it offers little more than a phantom picture of the processes that shaped man's past. What the moving finger has writ is no longer legible to later generations and was little enough known by the generations that were present at the writing. Too often it is assumed that the sketchy relics of indoctrinated contemporaries and the pious documents of state suffice to give a tolerably adequate basis for the interpretation of the past. The more popular histories are mostly concerned with events, the flagrant doings of dynasts, military victories and defeats, proclamations, manifestoes, treaties and so forth, whereas the changes of longer historic significance are motions and ferments in the underlying culture, changes that emerge and operate mostly in unobtrusive ways.

Man alone, of all created things known on this earth, has some capacity to shape his own future this way or that. His capacity to do so depends not solely on his understanding of external nature and his consequent power to utilize its forces but also on his ability to interpret his own history. It has some fairly obvious lessons to teach concerning the conditions of failure or success, of prosperity or adversity. But he is unready to study his own past with the same intelligence he applies to the study of nature. His prejudices and some of his cherished traditions stand in the way. Misrepresenting the past reality which he has no power to change, he misconceives the present reality over which he has some power.

Man lives by his values. Without them no society could endure. But values, too, are subject to the test of time. They must meet the challenge of changing conditions and changing needs. Societies that cannot adjust their values to the challenge lose out in the race and are eroded away. Perhaps we can say that the values and the value systems that successfully ride out the internal and external changes they experience are themselves of the stuff of reality. They prescribe relations between man and his environment that strengthen the bonds of community. They are the laws of the invisible reality of the spirit that dwells in man.

XIX

TIME, SPACE AND SPACE-TIME

Henceforth space in itself and time in itself
sink to mere shadows and only a sort of union
of the two preserves an independent existence.
—HERMANN MINKOWSKI,
on Einstein's space-time continuum.

IN THIS CHAPTER we again approach the edge of the unknown, but this time we follow a guideline that enables us to travel nearer to it than was possible a generation ago. We shall try to convey to the reader some indication of how the recent revolution in cosmic physics has expanded and changed the scientific viewpoint of the relation of time to the physical universe. The new viewpoint may not seem relevant to the time problems of this mortal life, but it offers a new perspective that requires us to change some of our common-sense ideas.

Our common-sense ideas serve us well enough for most practical affairs, but when we follow them to their limits we are likely to arrive at perplexities or even contradictions. Let us take one or two examples.

We have for convenience been speaking of time and space as similar principles, each applying exclusively over its own cosmic range. We think of them as the universal "containers" of all phenomena. Objects, we say, exist in space, and events happen in time. Objects are the filling of space without which it is empty, just as processes, or

111

changes of any sort, are the filling of time. Space gives one set of dimensions, breadth and length and height, and time another, as the measure of continuance or persistence. But we see no relationship between the two containers, between the dimensions of space and the dimensions of time. We don't think of time as being anything except that in which objects endure and change, and we don't think of space as anything except that in which objects find room to exist.

It is obvious, however, that all objects must exist both in space and in time. To exist in space objects must endure; they must then exist in time as well. To exist in time objects must exist somewhere; that is, they must exist in space as well. But how can that be so unless there is some relationship between space and time? Common sense fails us at this point.

We are baffled again when we raise the question whether the space and time universe is limited or unlimited. Infinity is beyond our conception. Somehow we can't think of space going on forever and ever and ever. Yet if we try to think of space as coming to an end, then it ends somewhere, and how can there be a boundary that is the boundary of nothing? Or if we try to think of time as having an ending, it must then have had a beginning; it must then have had a beginning *at some time,* which is a contradiction. And again common sense gives up the problem.

Thus far we have thought of time and space as though they presented parallel questions to us and fulfilled parallel roles within the cosmic order. In some respects, however, we do find what seem to be disparities between them. We mentioned at an early stage one such disparity. Time is for mortals a one-way street. All organic beings have a time of birth and undergo an irreversible process of aging. In space we move back or forth, and given the necessary impetus any movement may change its course in any direction. If we still retain the container idea, time thus seems a curious kind of container. We think of space as accommodating and open to our exploration but of time as binding—we have no power whatever to remain for one moment at the age we are at this moment. Time, unlike space, appears to us unidirectional as well as unidimensional. Strictly speaking, however, we should say not that time itself is unidimensional, but that *we* can move in only one direction through time.

Another apparent disparity is that whereas everything exists somewhere in time, now or then or always, non-material things do not seem to have any spatial existence. We may say thoughts and emotions exist in the mind, but does that mean they occupy any space? Thoughts are conveyed from mind to mind through material means of communication. Does the thought carried by the sound-waves or the radio waves occupy any space? Or take, say, a poem written on a piece of paper. It is not the ink or the paper. It exists only as a meaning conveyed by means of symbols. We cannot say even that it exists *in* the mind. Sometimes an inscribed tablet in an unknown language is unearthed. It conveys no meaning until some scholar finds a clue to the symbols on it, so that at length the tablet is interpreted. Nothing physical has been added, but it now yields its message. So in all modes of communication we have signs, images, figures, pictographs, material conveyers of a nonmaterial meaning. On a larger scale we can equally claim that a science, a religion, a legal code; in fact vast areas of the whole cultural realm have no spatial existence, though they certainly exist in time.

So far we have been concerned with common-sense de-liverances. As we see, they raise many problems and in some instances lead to a total impasse. But our outlook changes when we invoke the new scientific conception of the relation of time and space, according to which they no longer remain independent or apart. It marks a major advance in human understanding of these tremendous principles. It offers an answer to some of our questions, even if it raises some big new ones in turn.

The first major lead toward the new conception was given by a famous experiment conducted by two American scientists, the Michelson-Morley experiment, in which, using a new instrument devised by Albert Michelson, the interferometer, it was discovered that the velocity of light is the same whether the light is speeding in the direction of the earth's motion or at right angles to it. This conclusion was contrary to all expectation.

The Michelson-Morley experiment was a tremendous challenge to scientists. One of them, the Irishman G. F. FitzGerald, proposed the revolutionary hypothesis that matter actually contracted in the direction of its motion, a conclusion which would explain the Michelson-Morley phenomenon. And a Dutch physicist, H. A. Lorentz, suggested that this contraction was connected with the velocity of light.

There was no effective follow-up of these leads until the genius of Albert Einstein took hold of them. The upshot was his epoch-making theory of relativity. It would be out of place here to attempt any account of the vast sweep of a doctrine that for the first time brought into one coherent system so many cosmic categories that previously had remained independent and even insulated—matter, energy, space, time, gravitation and the velocity of light. Einstein not only modified and reinterpreted the long-established Newtonian system, but he also introduced a new perspective on the nature of the universe, setting a direction that top-level research in physics will be following up for generations to come.

For Newton time was absolute, unaffected by space or motion, moving onward in its imperturbable aloofness, with its endless succession of instantaneous presents endlessly disappearing into an infinite past. Likewise space was absolute, unaffected by time or motion, spreading on and on in every direction with mathematical integrity.

These common-sense assumptions bulwarked Newton's great conception of a cosmic order, with every star and every atom kept in its place by the law of gravitation and the laws of motion. It endured intact for centuries, because it admirably accounted for the motions of the heavenly bodies and for much else besides. But here and there a discrepancy, a seemingly small misfit, was discovered. The planet Mercury did not follow precisely the orbit the laws prescribed. Perhaps there was some unknown perturbing factor. And when one went down into the newly opening realm of the subatomic, some curious things happened that seemed to call for a different explanation. Perhaps there were different laws for these infinitesimals.

This last hypothesis proved indeed to be correct. Atoms and subatoms did not behave in accordance with Newton's mechanics. The quantum theory offered a profoundly different approach. But all that is another story. It was Einstein who came forward with the answer to Mercury's seeming misbehavior. It was Einstein who solved the problem posed by the Michelson-Morley experiment. In doing so he found a new constant, a quantitative fact that is in no way affected or changed by any relationships or by any other changes within the whole universe; and he showed that two other presumed constants, two realities hitherto held to be independent of conditions, were actually relative, one to the other. The new constant was the velocity of light, say 186,300 miles per second in free space. The two relative principles were space and time. You cannot specify the time of an event except in a particular system of space relationships or the place of an event except in a particular time system.

When you establish that a certain event occurred at a

certain time, what you have established is true within the system of reference in which you are. Two events that are simultaneous for you may not be simultaneous for someone else who is in motion relative to you. Two flashes of lightning, to take Einstein's own simplest example, may be simultaneous to you who are standing still at a point midway between the two flashes but actually will not be simultaneous for a passenger observing them at a point opposite you but on a moving train. To take a more surprising example, if a clock were sped to another star and then back to earth, the time it would register on its return would differ from that shown by a clock on earth that had been synchronized with the first clock. Likewise, if a yardstick were similarly conveyed through space it would become a trifle shorter while in such rapid motion. Mass itself varies according to its speed. But the velocity of light is unchanged so that it matters not whether the light emanates from a moving body or from a body at rest.

The profound reasoning embodied in Einstein's formulation of the theory of relativity and the complex calculations that sustained it lie outside our range, but the new insight it conveyed respecting the nature of the cosmos can in degree be appreciated by nonscientists. Abandoning as untenable the old constants of time and space, Einstein was able to fit several hitherto unrelated physical principles into a beautifully integrated system. In the famous equation $E=MC^2$ he stated the equivalence of energy and mass, E being the amount of energy and C^2, the enormous multiple, the square of the velocity of light. The velocity of light was not only a constant but one that played a comprehensive role in the structure of the universe. It was also a speed that could not under any conditions be exceeded by any other motion.

The full reach of the Einstein theory was extended in

his later general theory of relativity. Here gravitation itself becomes in effect an equivalent of inertia. And time
and space become a single four-dimensional order, the
space-time continuum in which all events are located.

We have ventured this most sketchy account of the
relativity doctrine not because it throws any direct light
on the time-focused problems of the life of man, but
because it can subtly modify some of our common pre-
conceptions about the meaning of time. Our vision of
the nature of the universe is thus enlarged. We comprehend a little better the magnificence of the order of the
cosmos, wherein nothing stands apart, but everything has
its established relation to everything else. We may even
speculate that all the marvelous attributes of the one universe may in the end be modes of one ultimate reality
nucleus. We may thus conclude that the human adventure,
so remarkable in its own kind, is also in intimate relationship with the grand design of the whole. Furthermore,
although the doctrine of relativity deals with the primal
constitutents of the cosmic order and may seem abstruse
and remote from the concerns of men, nevertheless its
new conception of time brings our human experience of
time more in accord with scientific theory. We have been
insisting that experienced time is not divided into the
sharp demarcations between past, present and future that
characterize the formalism of a mathematical system. The
present is not for the conscious being an instantaneous
exposure, a mere flash of actualized existence extinguished
immediately in the unbroken succession of flashes from
the unrolling future, like the series of photographs on the
whirring tape of a movie camera. The experienced present is a period of time of more or less duration, gliding
imperceptibly out of the past and merging smoothly into
the future. This perception is congenial to the theory
of the space-time continuum. Time is seamless in its

union with seamless space. Time is no longer the aloof regulator of events but conjunct with space in the frame of the universe.

For us, in our minute area of the space-time continuum, the span of the present embraces the mere edges of the time before us and behind. No doubt to a gnat the ambit of the present would be far narrower than ours. And we might conjecture that to an immortal mind the span would have no limit, so that our past and present and future would be one moment in its sight.

Coda

TIME AS MEASURED AND
TIME AS LIVED

> *And that old common arbitrator, Time . . .*
> —WILLIAM SHAKESPEARE, *Troilus and Cressida*

IN TWO VERY different ways time is of concern to us all. There is the time we measure, and there is the time we live. There is time as that which dates all happenings, and there is time as that within which potency realizes itself, vitality fulfills itself, experience grows and expresses itself.

Under the former aspect time is treated as a recorder, marking the stages of every process and registering the happenings of every now, each now being the line of the recording tape over which the needle is passing on its endless way. The tape itself is graduated with inconceivable fineness. It enables us to set in order all the items of knowledge we discover about anything or everything in the whole changing universe. It is used to regulate the behavior of all our mechanisms. Without it we could not do any planning, any organizing, any efficient purposing.

119

The recording tape is therefore an eminently service-able device, but it is still purely a measuring instrument. It tells us nothing about what it records. It records only the markings on the surface of change and consequently tells us little enough about the true concern of history, the manner in which change itself is the response and the manifestation of the subject of change.

The graduations of the moving tape are used to mark birthdays and other anniversaries, seasonal beginnings and endings, the progression of all cyclical motions up to aeonian periodicity of the orbits of cosmic systems. The tapeline determines our risings and our retirings and often enough our spells of work and leisure. It chronicles the commencement of all enterprises, the culmination of all achievements, the closing of all books. It sets the signal for prayers and for wedding bells and for the funeral toll. The prisoner "does time" as measured by it. We project on the lines of the tape the schedule of our to-be-fulfilled programs.

The more complex our civilization becomes, the more insistent and rigorous are the allocations we make for the yet unrolled tape. Only so can the many threads of the multiple activities and objectives of an interdependent society be woven into a pattern. Only so can we space its calls for incessant meetings, consultations, routinized procedures, assembly-line functionings, reportings, arrivings, departings, accountings and settlements.

Time as measured may then become a tyrant, violating the natural tempo, the organic habituation, the psychic readiness and substituting for it a mechanized determinant of our responses, of our comings and goings, of our modes of operation and even of our modes of thought. The date book becomes the master of the master and the punch clock the master of the servant. We rise not when we are refreshed and ready for the day but when the alarm sounds. We eat not when we are hungry but when the timetable dictates. We may feel like prolonging an activity we are pursuing with enjoyment but must turn to another because it is next on the schedule. We may want to take more time for reflection on a troublesome problem, but the calendar calls for a decision. We hustle uncomfortably because there is a date line to meet.

There is truth in the indictment but by no means the whole truth. Often enough we can make virtues of our necessities instead of falling the victims of them. The simple society has usually been the needy society, wherein the mere struggle to exist is a far more stringent and hopeless necessity than the requisite conformity to a schedule. Moreover, the geared efficiency that makes the time schedule necessary not only makes work vastly more productive but also shortens the working day, opening up new areas of resourceful leisure unknown to former generations.

Our concern with the clock and the calendar has, however, other dangers for us. Time as measured may become the enemy of time as lived. So long as our eyes keep observing the clock, we cannot feel free; we cannot immerse ourselves in the savor of being and of doing. A highly successful man of affairs remarked to the writer that he did not require his office staff to punch the clock morning or evening, because he wanted them to feel they were co-workers with himself. Unfortunately, he added, this arrangement is not feasible in a very big plant.

On a broader scale the scrupulous calculation of time spent has a cramping effect on the spirit. The precise accounting of the calendar of age instills the consciousness of the steady dwindling of the life course yet to run, causing fears of the future to darken the opportunities of the present and to diminish the edge of our remaining joys. Moreover, calendar age is associated with traditions and proprieties emanating from a time when the expectation of life was much lower, when the period of vigor was considerably shorter, when, for example, the grandmother was an old crone who occupied the armchair by the hearth, her active days being ended.

To recognize the brevity of life is not at issue here. This recognition—which in no way requires the meticulous counting of the passing hours and days—is a spur to the evocation of the quality of living. Time is for mortals a precious possession with which it is wise to be neither spendthrift nor miserly. Some sense of limits is necessary for the art of living which, like all other arts, must express itself in significant design within the compass appropriate to the creative powers of the artist. Only infinite being has any use for infinite time. The time limitation within which man must manifest the art of living may be all too short, but its brevity must be related to the limits of his powers. Were there no such limits, his emotions would languish and his purposes fade. Why be eager now if there is unlimited time ahead? The sting of living, the poignancy of experience, the appreciation of beauty, the urge to endeavor, the impetus of desire, the joy of attainment and the tragedy of defeat would all dwindle into insignificance. The creative spirit, unable to identify itself for lack of direction, like a traveler who gets nowhere because all roads lead everywhere, would be dissipated and would decay into routine, into the undifferentiated expression of material law, undistinguished from the responsiveness to it of a grain of dust or of a star.

These considerations suggest the need for the free cultivation of capacity, an approach that is very different from the attitude that narrowly metes out the hours and the hastening days. To be overconcerned with the passage of the years is to numb the freedom with which we live them as they pass. And to make the clock the arbiter of the precise period we allot to each undertaking, to turn the current of our attention on and off as we turn the switch of an electric battery, because our schedule is so arranged, is to reduce our power to enjoy and become absorbed in our activities. For purely routine operations the regulator is expedient, but for any commitments we find worthwhile in themselves it is a sheer intrusion.

Actually, no matter how neatly proportioned is the timing set for us by the organization of our working day, the attention and energy we direct to it rise and fall in some kind of variant rhythm, not only within the day but also within the weeks and the months, with intervals that may mount to excitation and others that may sink to boredom. No artificial timing can determine the motions of the mind. And when our interest is thoroughly aroused, we have a sense of living, a union of work with life, that makes us regardless of the ticking of the clock.

In sum, the quality of living expresses itself in free organic rhythms that reject the mechanics of the time schedule. Here, as elsewhere in the economy of living, wherever we emphasize quantity we depreciate quality. It is perhaps a sign of the times, an illegitimate transference from the vast significance of calculation and refined measurement in such triumphant physical projects as the exploration of space, that geometrical abstractions have attained such prominence in the fine arts and that quantitative summations have won such a barren vogue in the social sciences. Creativeness has been cramped into alien confines within which it is often reduced to ingenuity. The vital difference that characterizes all organic nature is ignored.

Among aggravated manifestations of the same tendency we would include the mode of reckoning in accordance with which certain experts, whether in military or in political science, contemplate the prospect of atomic warfare. In quantitative terms it differs from conventional warfare only in degree. It would wipe out hundreds of millions instead of tens and would incapacitate more hundreds of millions instead of a fraction of that number and would

destroy a vast portion of the accumulated wealth of mankind and of the artistic and cultural heritage of all the
past. But, they calculate, there would remain a balance in
favor of one side, and so devastating a war would necessarily be of short duration, and the rate of reproduction always increases after a war—and so on complacently to a
Q.E.D. These strategists do not inquire how so ruinous a
cataclysm might be related to any objectives for the sake of
which presumably the war was waged by either side. Nor
does it seem to occur to them that the difference they
reckon in degrees may be for humanity a difference of
kind. For if human beings were exposed to the blasting annihilation of all that made life dear to them, survivors in a
wilderness of rubble and disease, what thereafter happened
to them might make a tale for the distant gods but would
have no relation whatever to the time calculations of the
experts of a buried age.

We might avoid some baseless fears and more than a
few delusions did we pay more respect to time as lived than
to time as measured. After all, the main reason why in our
everyday affairs we measure time is because we are concerned with the distribution of it; our time is our book of
days, days already lived and days awaiting to be lived. If
the filling of the page that now lies open for us wholly occupies us, we do not count the lines or measure the para-
graphs. It is the unlived hours, the balked hours, the hours
of unwilling toil or of frustrated energy, the minutes of
which drag on. When instead we are in love with what life
offers or promises, we ride on the wave of organic time,
letting it carry us forward as it will. The going can be
rough; sometimes we get bruised and shaken, but we have
accepted the challenge and are ready to take it as it comes.

The strong feel of being redeems us from the fear of
time. While it endures, the time is our time, our precious
possession.

Imagine being shipwrecked, a lone survivor on an empty

island to which had floated ample ship's supplies for months of existence. One has nothing to do. The dreary sun crawls across the sky. An intolerable sense of vacancy, of total bereftness, takes hold as one vainly scans the sea day after day. The lost, unused days are followed by troubled, foreboding nights.

Suppose, however, that one moonless night the solitary discerns on the black horizon a faint pinpoint of light. A ship? A star? The light remains motionless, though he watches for hours. It must mean land, he concludes, another island—and an inhabited one, whose low-lying coast he had failed to see on the hazy horizon.

The sea, the island, the aloneness are as before, but the man is utterly changed. Time no longer hangs on his hands. Purpose has come back to him and renewed the feel of life. He plans a fire signal for the next night. He plans the making of a raft, using driftwood and bits of trees and strips of bark and lengths of a stringy vine. We need not carry the illustration further. It is all obvious enough: When one's days are filled with an engrossing purpose, one has the sense of time redeemed, of time lived.

Occasionally one reads a press report concerning some elderly person who has just received the only kind of special recognition that comes to those who have lived unobtrusive lives of quiet service, the assembling of his friends to celebrate his retirement or some advanced anniversary. And when the guest of honor finally rises to respond to the toast of his health, his remarks take the following turn: "I have been a teacher" (or, say, a country doctor or a postmaster or a craftsman of some kind) "the greater part of my days and I have never regretted it. I enjoyed my work, the opportunities it gave me for service, the friendships it brought me. I have had my troubles, but as I look back on it all, I can say with a thankful heart it was a good life." It was his testimony that he had lived his time.

We live part of our time, and we live through the rest. The proportion depends on many things but mostly on what we are and what we have become. We live our life when we exchange it for worthwhile experience, for experience that absorbs and satisfies. There is no one criterion for experience that is worthwhile. We are variantly constituted, and what absorbs the heart and mind of one may fail to move another. Perhaps the only partial test is that the experience must appear good in retrospect when it has worked itself out in its fruits. There are high moments of experience, whatever our lot otherwise may have been, whatever the range of our potentialities, when the life spirit takes full possession of us. It is as though all unknowingly we had reached a mountain top and seen below us the wonder of the earth, as it never appears to our ordinary sight. And when we have descended, we say in effect: It was good for us to have been there. And the memory bequeaths something to many quieter hours, conveying the sense that our time is no longer being lived through but being lived.

TIME, MYSELF AND MY WORK

"IF HOPES were dupes, fears may be liars." These lines are peculiarly appropriate to our hopes and fears concerning time. And when our fears are liars our hopes have generally been misplaced. Looking back over a long life span, as I now do, I can recall so many false fears: fears that when youth passes the zest goes out of living; fears that one's middle age will be weighed down with cares; fears that old age will be weary and painful and joyless—all the half-unuttered fears that at each stage of life lead us to misconceive the years to come. Actually each stage of life has its own satisfactions as well as its own problems, and looking back again, I cannot feel that the satisfactions of youth were greater or its problems less serious than those of later periods. I believe that often when we wish we could be young again, it is not because the joys of youth were actually greater but because with youth we have more life yet to come. The urge to live on is our deepest instinct and remains unshaken as long as life is anyway tolerable.

The future is always a question mark, but we fill its unknown sky with shadowy misconceptions that cause us present worries. Some of these worries are centered in our personal affairs, and there the only proper substitute for worry is a combination of intelligent (but not excessive) planning and faith. But other worries spring from our misconceptions about time itself, about the flight of time, about time and the process of living. It is with respect to these worries that the saying properly applies: "Take no thought for the morrow; for the morrow shall take thought for the things of itself. Sufficient unto the day is the evil thereof."

With these misconceptions about time I have dealt, directly or indirectly, in this book. Let me try to illustrate some of them, and some answers to them, from my own experience.

To begin with, since change is incessant everywhere—in our successes and failures, in our various relationships, in our workaday situations, in the economic and political conditions that concern us all, in our own inmost thoughts—there are occasions when the impermanence, the instability, the insecurity of our lives and fortunes give us a melancholy sense of the frailty of all things mortal. This feeling has come to me under very different circumstances: on hearing of the unexpected death of an old friend; or in some early morning reverie that brought back a once familiar scene now almost forgotten; or on visiting after many years the little town where I was born and finding myself unknown where once I had been so much at home; or in a time of war when all the kindly usages of happier days were swept aside, and there seemed no end to the sorrowful destruction. Then the very ground on which we stood became a shifting sand. The reflection is natural and salutary enough, but the mood it engenders should not be perpetuated—as it does become with some authors of our own day—into a philosophy of life.

In periods of personal unsettlement we may recover a sense of proportion if we realize that change itself is experienced only against the background of what endures. The clouds scurry across the enduring sky; the waves surge on over the enduring sea. For ourselves we need to discover the abiding realities that are also ours. In this discovery lies our assurance and also, at need, our consolation. Throughout the ages men have found in religion the main basis of assurance. But ours is an age of half-beliefs and absence of beliefs with respect to any specific religious faith, and so for many of us our anchorage in time must be our enduring interests and our basis of enduring relationships. Subject to change and to loss as they are in the course of time, they are value-laden, and if the values are strong and high, they too participate in the quality of religion, of the enduring value that permeates the nature of things.

There are various ways in which we thus can find the immutable, the immutable for *us,* in the midst of change.

Here I may appeal to my own experience. I belong to the number of those who have a variety of working interests, some more intimate and deeper than others. Sustaining these interests there are my social interests, family, companions, friends. Most of my working day is reasonably congenial, for it lies in the field of learning, researching, some teaching. But there are still stretches within it that are not fully engrossing, that leave me with the sense of unfulfillment. Then I find release, an inward satisfaction, in retreating to my study and setting down my reflections on the larger questions of human existence and this feeling toward the timeless. The deep satisfaction of it is accompanied by some travail, for this thinking and writing do not come nearly so easily as the normal work of a scholar. The satisfaction is purely an inner one, for I neither anticipate nor in fact achieve any special recognition as a result of the end product. In passing I may remark that the present book also comes from these periods of retreat.

Everyone needs to find his own mode of communion with the timeless, with what for him remains secure beyond the chances and vicissitudes of time. In that area, whether it lie in the religious realm or in any system of primary values or in devotion to any cause, he must in his

times of retreat find there the deepest satisfaction in life—
or else it will fail him in the end.

As for our everyday preoccupations with the ceaseless
erosion of our time, I have found that it helps to create a
more healthy outlook when one dispels certain prevalent
misconceptions. In the early chapters of this book I dwelt
on the commonest of these misconceptions. Time itself
does nothing to us—it doesn't hurry us or speed away from
us. It is not time that brings us wrinkles or gray hairs. We
are born with a fund of undeveloped energies and multiple
potentialities, remarkable, even amazing potentialities, as
the history of mankind has shown, but they are limited,
and the vital energies are at length used up, as all expended
energies are. Time is then simply in this respect the period
in which we develop and utilize and enjoy the use of our
fund. We can use it more wisely and thus conserve its resources longer, and the advance of medical science gives us
strong hope that the initial fund can be made to last longer
before it is all expended. I cannot quite say why I find this
way of looking on time—this more correct way—somewhat more comforting. But there it is.

There is another aspect of our energy fund I find even
more comforting. We know that sheer physical prowess is
relatively short-lived, that, for example, a boxer is already
old for his job in his early thirties and that an athlete generally can compete successfully only in his younger days,
possibly up to the age of forty. But it is very different with
our fund of mental energy, with the potentialities of intellectual achievement and also with our emotional experience in at least many of its expressions. Moreover, the
ambitions of human beings, the urges for place, prestige,
power in particular, so far from losing their vitality, seem
often to become only stronger in age. This may be for better or worse so far as its effect on society is concerned, but
at least the urge maintains the zest for living in those whom

it animates. In a word, experience suggests that many of the enjoyments of life, so long as health is fairly well maintained, do not languish or even diminish as one advances in years.

It follows that one of the best preparations for the enjoyment of later life is the development in youth of a genuine interest in intellectual pursuits, in cultural studies, in the appreciation of the arts or of the finer crafts, so that knowledge of beauty of form, rhythm, line, color, harmony, design, or of the wisdom, expressiveness, vision, imagination of the great thinkers and writers of the ages become one's own inheritance. I count myself most fortunate that I was brought up in a home where the value of learning and the worth of the great books were inculcated and that I found myself responsive to the inculcation, so that I had always an active interest in knowledge as well as a treasure house to which in later years I could retreat. Along this road, at its various stages, I have found at intervals an entire absorption, sometimes in reading a book that proved wholly congenial or else intellectually stimulating, more often in the retreat where one wrestles to make clearer one's thoughts on the more enduring things—so that the time was wholly lived and thereby redeemed. But there are many roads that can lead different minds and different dispositions to this goal.

It must not, of course, be supposed that any human being, no matter how devoted, no matter how happily situated, can ever live all, or even a majority, of his waking hours within this sheer experience of full engrossment. We must spend many hours in the valley and on the rising slopes before we ascend to a peak, but having been there we have a vision that stays with us. There are many hours of quiet living, of rest and relaxation, of adventures by the way, hours also of trial and struggle and of crisis. But the experience of our fully satisfying hours can radiate into the rest and help to sustain the sense that life is indeed worth-while. In a not dissimilar vein Euripides, in one of his wonderful dramatic choruses, reflected:

> Whoe'er can know,
> As the long days go,
> That *to live is happy*
> Hath found his heaven.[1]

What does it mean then to enjoy this sense of fulfillment, of time that is really lived, nor merely passed through? The problem we have been viewing from the angle of time is the universal problem that men have approached from various other angles: What makes life worth while? What gives us the sense that life is for us, for you or for me, really worth while? The answers offered have been themselves various and conflicting. But whatever they are, whether they find salvation through a way of believing, a way of doing or a way of feeling, they have all had at their base a common element. The way they prescribe must enlist the personality in wholehearted unison with some reality that absorbs and fulfills the being. The fulfillment of personality is thus a form of communion, whether it be with the God a man worships; or with nature under some aspect; or through intimate communication with ideal things, the inexhaustible quality of beauty or truth that pervades the universe; or with some cause that calls into action all one's power; or even with things of lesser significance so long as they suffice to satisfy the human craving for union. As I muse over my own hours of fullest experience, I realize that it was always in the active presence of what for me was precious and intrinsic reality.

To live well one must come to terms with the inevitable. Within that order comes our determinate course through time. In this book I have set out, looking back over the

---

[1] Translated by Gilbert Murray.

years, some thoughts that have arisen in my own encounter with time, thoughts about the ways men have responded to its challenge and thoughts about the ways in which, according to our opportunities, we can live well in reasonable adjustment to its inevitability. Most of us, it seems to me, refuse to face the issue. We are merely uneasy about it, beset by doubts and fears. So at best we make a partial and insecure accommodation to it. We can do better than that.